The Lighthouse Keeper's Wife

Connie Scovill Small, Avery Rock, *circa* 1923.

THE LIGHTHOUSE
KEEPER'S WIFE

by Connie Scovill Small

THE UNIVERSITY OF MAINE PRESS

IN ASSOCIATION WITH
FRIENDS OF PORTSMOUTH
HARBOR LIGHTHOUSES

The Lighthouse Keeper's Wife is published by

University of Maine Press
5729 Fogler Library
Orono, ME 04469
www.umaine.edu/umpress/

in association with

Friends of Portsmouth Harbor Lighthouses
A chapter of the American Lighthouse Foundation
P.O. Box 8232
Portsmouth, NH 03802-8232
https://www.portsmouthharborlighthouse.org

The University of Maine Press is a division of The Raymond H. Fogler Library.

This edition was first published 1999, this printing 2019.

Paper used in this publication meets the minimum requirements of the American National Standard for Information Sciences — Permanence of Paper for Printed Library Materials, ANSI Z39.48-1984.

Printed in the United States by Cushing-Malloy, Inc., Ann Arbor, MI 48104
Book design by Michael Alpert.

Cover photograph: Portsmouth Harbor Lighthouse, by Jeremy D'Entremont.

ISBN: 978-0-89101-098-2 (paperback — revised edition)

TABLE OF CONTENTS

ILLUSTRATIONS

Frontispiece: Connie Scovill Small, Avery Rock, *circa* 1923

Map of significant places 2

A gallery of photographs follows page 26
(all photographs courtesy of Connie Scovill Small)

Dedicated to the memory of Elson Small
and to my good friend Ruth Bunker Ellis

Connie Scovill Small (born 4 June 1901) first published her autobiography, *The Lighthouse Keeper's Wife*, in 1986 at the age of eighty-five. It was, in part, the fruition of an idea seeded in 1947, when Connie and her husband Elson retired after twenty-eight years of lighthouse living and service along the Maine and New Hampshire coasts. But more immediately, it was written in response to a thoughtless remark that pierced the depth of Connie's soul: "How on earth could anyone have any kind of a life in a lighthouse?" (169). Connie's answer is a genuine, insightful, and compelling narrative about a most meaningful kind of a life of "people risking their own lives to help men and ships; a life of order and duty" (156).

By using autobiography to tell about her life in lighthouses, Connie Small joins a literary heritage of women authors who have established a tradition of American women's autobiography.[1] While all women do not have a common identity, they share a common socially constructed perspective; thus, the way women have written about their lives is different from the way men have written about their lives. A good example of this difference is Connie and Elson themselves. Since he was, according to Connie, "the participator" and concerned himself with the public affairs on shore and she was "an observer" concerned with domestic affairs, Elson Small would have written a very different autobiography about life in a lighthouse than she did. (124) He surely would not have chosen a title for his life history that reflected his conception of himself as focused on his relationship to another person.[2] Yet, Connie, like many other women writers in the modern period, represents herself in the title of her autobiography by her relationship to another.[3] She presents herself, simply, as the lighthouse keeper's wife.

Estelle C. Jelinek convincingly argues from her research that there is a "literary history of the characteristics in women's self-writings, which contemporary autobiographers continue."[4] Connie Small's autobiography does indeed incorporate a number of these characteristics. First, the emphasis of her narrative is on personal matters — family, her marriage, friends, and domestic activities. This is in contrast to traditional men's autobiographies that emphasize military and political accomplishments. Second, like other women autobiographers, Connie wrote her self-history because she felt a need for authentication. Living in a lighthouse made her unusual, even exotic, as in Connie's words, "because we were living on an island, [tourists] gave us to understand we were some sort of freaks." (85; 123) Especially after the comment by a thoughtless club woman, she felt a need to justify her worth; to show pride in and to document her successful life of order and duty. And third, Connie's writing style and form also conform to a tradition of women's autobiography. While she attempts to tell her story chronologically, she interrupts her narrative with anecdotes, character sketches, and flashbacks. A wonderful example of this is Chapter Three, in which we meet Grandmother Myers; travel to France, Sweden, Canada, and Holland; attend Connie and Elson's wedding; learn to cook on a black iron Atlantic coal stove in the middle of the Bay of Fundy; and move to Avery Rock light house. This "disjunctiveness" is, in Jelinek's analysis, a literary style particular to women's life studies and it "documents not the events of their times but the emotional conscience of America."[5]

Autobiographies are problematic. They are often written when people are older and memories are dimmed; life experiences and loved ones are understandably shown only in the best light; and what is written and not written is subjective and selective. All that said, *The Lighthouse Keeper's Wife* is an important primary source for understanding New England's maritime history in general and women's history in particular. Connie's autobiography documents a way of life that has all but disappeared since the automation of lighthouses. It was a life that combined "home and the sea" (44) and this gave it a pre-industrial sense long into the twentieth century. With her autobiography, Connie has given us invaluable details about the historical material culture of food, shelter, and clothing; descriptions of personal working and recreation experiences; and a rare glimpse of particular attitudes, values, and beliefs from another time.

While there was a traditional division of labor by sex on the lighthouses — Connie did all the housework, cooking, and domestic chores (without electricity or plumbing!) and Elson did maintenance, tended the light, and was their link to the mainland — work duties were often blurred. As Connie explains, if the lighthouse keeper was ill, or had to go to shore, "a member of the family was expected to take over; no extra money was paid for this service" (74). In fact lighthouse keeping was officially considered a family affair by the lighthouse service, and as one historian contends, they shrewdly made use of the free labor families could provide.[6] Lighthouse keeping is one of the best historical illustrations of women's "double day" magnified — working both for the government and in their homes for no pay.

Yet, lighthouse service also gave women economic opportunities. Many wives and daughters in the nineteenth century took over the duties of their deceased husbands or fathers. They often received

official appointments because there was no pension system to care for them. The fifth auditor of the Treasury Department,

Stephen Pleasonton, responsible for lighthouse service from 1820 [to] 1852 was comfortable with appointing women keepers, and felt that widows and daughters of keepers were particularly worthy candidates for their position.[7]

From 1828 to 1905, over one hundred women in the United States were appointed official keepers in their own names and about four hundred were officially appointed assistant keepers.[8] Though not officially named as such, Connie was, without a doubt, a co-lighthouse keeper. One district superintendent in the 1930s surely had Connie Small in mind when he commented, "I know of no other branch of government service in which the wife plays such an important part."[9]

Most poignant in Connie's autobiography is her honest examination of her long marriage and her willingness to share its workings. One reason we read autobiographies is their relevance to our own lives; thus, we yearn to learn from Connie how one makes a relationship or marriage successful. How does one retain the integrity of their individualism in a community of two? Literary critic Carolyn Heilbrun states that for women throughout history, "adulthood — marriage or spinsterhood — implied relative loss of self."[10] While Connie and Elson accepted traditional gender roles and responsibilities in their marriage, Connie always kept a sense of who she was — she never lost herself. She just made certain conscious choices and is frank about what she gave in order to make her marriage successful.

> I think the reason Elson and I were so close and so happy was that I put inside of me my desires, my longings, things I wanted to do, if they came in conflict with what he wanted. I felt what I wanted were selfish desires. I knew later they weren't selfish, but I didn't think so then and one or the other had to give, so I gave and I've never been sorry. (112)

These themes of true love and sacrifice either for another person or one's duty in the lighthouse service resonate throughout Connie's autobiography. As Connie discovered, like her mother, and grandmother, and great-grandmother before her, fulfillment and purpose in life can come from giving.

It was the training in the lighthouses that gave Connie the strength and courage to continue her life of order and duty in unexpected ways on her own (162). That training started the first time she went to Channel Light as Elson's wife. In the middle of some of the strongest tidal waters in the world, Connie looked up at thirty feet of black iron ladder she was sure she could never climb. "Oh yes, you can. Just grab the rungs and I'll be right behind you," encouraged Elson.

> So, with him behind me telling me to look up and never down, I made it. To this day I have kept his words with me and when I'd get discouraged I would think of them. They've helped me a good many times to overcome a panicky feeling and do what had to be done. (35)

"Look up and never down" helped Connie to face the "panicky feeling" of an economic future without the pension from the Coast Guard that she was rightfully due after Elson's death. It gave her the courage to get a license for the first time at the age of fifty-nine and to drive herself to her new career as a head resident at Farmington (Maine) State College. Never forgetting what it means to feel the inevitable isolation, loneliness and uncertainty of living, Connie continues to give of herself by passing these life-saving words, "Look up and never down," on to all who meet her.

Lighthouses hold a powerful attraction for people. While they are reminders of our architectural and economic heritage, they symbolize faithfulness, steadfastness, clarity, and hope. Connie's autobiography captures the essence of the lighthouse experience:

> Now, I never see a light shining from these beacons but I am filled with a sense of peace and security, a sense of trust that has gladdened the hearts of sailors all over the world for more than two thousand years. (6)

Thus, like lighthouses themselves, her book holds a powerful attraction for people as well. Since it was published, Connie has given close to five hundred presentations about her experiences. One of the highlights of her life was an invitation in 1993 to speak to doctors and medical students as part of the Geriatric Celebrity series at Case Western University in Cleveland, Ohio, about taking care of medical problems and emergencies while living in an isolated lighthouse. They were, said Connie, "very much interested in how the use of common sense and intelligence created the wisdom to solve whatever problems occurred."[11]

Because Connie's presentation of her unique life history is so captivating, she has been interviewed for numerous newspaper and magazine articles and she has participated in several important television documentaries. She was featured in *Light Spirit*, a video narrated by Jack Perkins that was used as a major fundraiser by New England Public Broadcasting stations. She stared in the popular National Public Broadcasting series called *Legendary Lighthouses of Maine* and she was highlighted in the PBS book, *Legendary Lighthouses*. Recently, Connie was recognized by *Good Housekeeping* in a tribute book as an important woman born at the turn of the century, and she was honored by a luncheon invitation from First Lady Hillary Rodham Clinton.[12] But, according to Connie, one of her proudest achievements to date is her work in preserving and restoring lighthouses:

> A great moment in my life occurred in 1997 when President George Bush recognized my work and life when he spoke at the Maine Lights Program in Northport, Maine. President Bush was referring to his One Thousand Points of Light when he said, "The torch is being passed from those who for more than two centuries have served and endured along the rugged Maine seashore in service to others. People like Connie Small and her late husband Elson, *we salute you.*"[13]

An essential and consistent element of all autobiography is the writer's sense that telling one's life story will be useful to others.[14] Connie hopes that her autobiography will encourage and inspire us to attempt a meaningful existence on our own terms so that we might know the same comfort at sunset "of a day well spent" that she has known. (170) Connie Scovill Small is proud of her life; it was and continues to be one of profound utility and is worthy of being examined through autobiography. Yet it is much more. *The Lighthouse Keeper's Wife* gives us the "magical opportunity of entering another life" as Jill Ker Conway suggests, that "really sets us thinking about our own."[15]

– Andrea Constantine Hawkes
18 June 1999

NOTES

1. See Estelle C. Jelinek. *The Tradition of Women's Autobiography: From Antiquity to the Present.* (Boston: Publishers, 1986); Bell Brodzki and Celeste Schenck, editors. *Life/Lines: Theorizing Women's Autobiography.* (Ithaca and London: Cornell University Press, 1988); Margo Culley, editor. American *Women's Autobiography: Fea(s)ts of Memory.* (Madison, Wisconsin: The University of Wisconsin Press, 1992).

2. For an in-depth discussion of this gender theory see the now classic works of: Nancy Chodorow, *The Reproduction of Mothering: Psychoanalysis and the Sociology of Gender* (Berkeley: University of California Press, 1978); and Carol Gilligan, *In a Different Voice: Psychological Theory and Women's Development* (Cambridge, Mass.: Harvard University Press, 1982).

3. Culley, *American Women's Autobiography*, 7–8.

4. Jelinek, *The Tradition of Women's Autobiography*, xii. This paragraph is based on Jelinek's analysis, xii–xiii; 102–104.

5. Ibid., 104.

6. Mary Louise Clifford and J. Candace Clifford. *Women Who Kept the Lights: An Illustrated History of Female Lighthouse Keepers*. (Williamsburg, Virginia: Cypress Communications, 1993), 2.

7. Ibid.

8. Ibid.

9. Bill Caldwell. *Lighthouses of Maine*. (Portland, Maine: Gannett Books, 1986), 260.

10. Carolyn G. Heilbrun, "Non-Autobiographies of 'Privileged' Women: England and America" in Brodzki and Schenck, *Life/Lines*, 72.

11. From private correspondence with author.

12. See *A Good Housekeeping Tribute, We Remember: Women Born at the Turn of the Century Tell the Stories of their Lives in Words and Pictures. By Jeanne Marie Laskas; Photographs by Lynn Johnson; Intro by Hillary Rodham Clinton. (New York: William Morrow & Co., 1999)*.

13. From private correspondence with author.

14. Culley, *American Women's Autobiography*, 14. See also, Jill Ker Conway. *When Memory Speaks: Reflections on Autobiography*. (New York: Alfred A. Knopf, 1998), 16.

15. Conway, *When Memory Speaks*, 18.

Thank you Michael, Celeste, and of course, Connie.

The Lighthouse Keeper's Wife

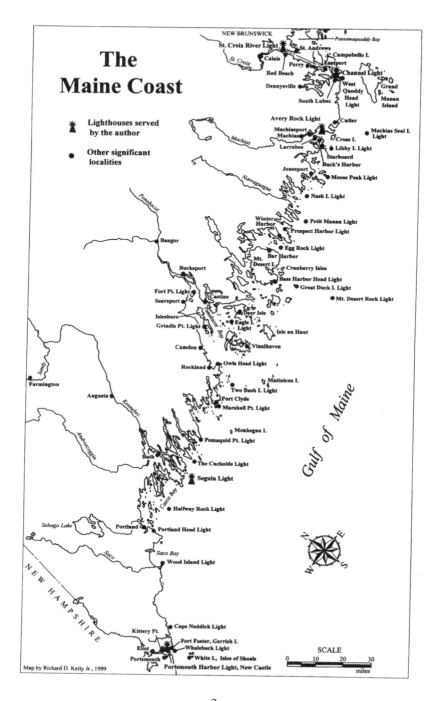

The
Maine Coast

🔆 Lighthouses served
   by the author

● Other significant
   localities

NEW BRUNSWICK
Passamaquoddy Bay
St. Croix River Light
St. Andrews
St. Croix
Calais
Campobello I.
Perry
Eastport
Red Beach
Channel Light
Dennysville
West
Quoddy
Head
Light
Grand
Manan
Island
South Lubec
Avery Rock Light
Cutler
Machias
Machiasport
Machias
Machias Seal I. Light
Cross I.
Larrabee
Libby I. Light
Starboard
Buck's Harbor
Jonesport
Narraguagus
Moose Peak Light
Nash I. Light
Penobscot
Winter
Harbor
Petit Manan Light
Prospect Harbor Light
Bangor
Egg Rock Light
Bar Harbor
Mt.
Desert I.
Cranberry Isles
Bucksport
Bass Harbor Head Light
Great Duck I. Light
Fort Pt. Light
Castine
Searsport
Mt. Desert Rock Light
Islesboro
Deer Isle
Grindle Pt. Light
Eagle I.
Light
Isle au Haut
Camden
Vinalhaven
Rockland
Owls Head Light
Matinicus I.
Farmington
Two Bush I. Light
Augusta
Kennebec
Port Clyde
Marshall Pt. Light
Androscoggin
Monhegan I.
Pemaquid Pt. Light
Bath
The Cuckolds Light
Gulf of Maine
Seguin Light
Casco Bay
Halfway Rock Light
Sebago Lake
Portland
Portland Head Light
Saco
Saco Bay
Wood Island Light
NEW HAMPSHIRE
Kittery Pt.
Cape Neddick Light
Fort Foster, Gerrish I.
Eliot
Whaleback Light
Portsmouth
White I., Isles of Shoals
Portsmouth Harbor Light, New Castle

SCALE
0   10   20   30
miles

Map by Richard D. Kelly Jr., 1999

ONE

FAREWELL TO PORTSMOUTH
LIGHTHOUSE

The dreaded day was here. My husband Elson and I had kept lighthouses along the Maine coast for twenty-eight years. Now, on this May day of 1948 we would put out the light for the last time, and I would go ashore to live another kind of life.

The bedroom light came on and woke me up. Elson loomed large in the door. He waited as I rubbed my eyes and got out of bed. It was 3:34 and sunrise would be at 4:20. Elson's standing there meant he was inviting me to go with him since it was the last time. He looked at his watch and said, "Take your time." I said, "Well, I can't wear just any old thing."

Elson had already showered, shaved, and dressed for the day. I washed, put on my prettiest summer outfit, checked my hair in the mirror to see if it was neat and becoming, and went down the stairs to Elson, who was waiting for me. Crossing the stone patio, we went up the few steps that took us through the stone wall of the fort and walked down the plank walk to the tower of the lighthouse.

Elson opened the big iron door. We climbed the winding, scrolled, iron stairs to the utility deck and then the ladder into the lantern. He opened a little side door and we squeezed through, Elson having a harder time than I because of his long legs. We breathed in the fresh ocean air as we walked around the catwalk of the lighthouse tower.

The sky was streaked with rainbow colors, the sea calm, the whole area asleep. It was still. I looked down forty feet to the little white scallops of incoming tide washing over the rocks, caressing each one lovingly.

Here at the Fort Point Lighthouse at Fort Constitution we had almost an aerial view of the pretty town of New Castle, New Hampshire. We could look up the Piscataqua River to Portsmouth with its gleaming white belfry of North Church, a landmark for sailors, silhouetted against the sky.

We could see also the Piscataqua River Bridge, built in memory of World War I veterans, which connected the states of New Hampshire and Maine. Across the bridge was the town of Kittery and the Portsmouth Naval Shipyard on Seavey Island. From the shipyard my eyes went to Kittery Point and to Fort Foster on Gerrish Island, a very active fort during World War II. Extending out about a mile to Wood Island were the pilings that had held the nets to prevent enemy submarines from entering the harbor. At the center of the harbor was Whaleback Lighthouse, and ten miles out to sea from that was the lighthouse on White Island, part of the Isles of Shoals. Both sent their beams across the water. My eyes then went back to Wood Island where the Coast Guard station was located.

Elson had planned to spend the rest of his service before retiring at Fort Point Lighthouse, or New Castle Light as it was called locally. We had been there only two years when the Coast Guard decided to move its station from Wood Island to the mainland. The house we lived in was to be made into the station, and that meant that I had to move while Elson remained there. Today was the day I was to leave, to say good-bye to twenty-eight years of lighthouse living.

As we stood looking at the sight we had come to love, Elson knew the sadness I felt at leaving. He said, "Don't think about it. Just keep on making plans." I looked out to the two lights and a Navy ship that had appeared on the horizon, trying to organize my feelings, thinking, "Yes, I'm sad to leave. I feel I'm leaving a large part of me to the sea, to the ships that depended on the lights we tended. Also, I'm scared, for I don't know as I can cope with this new way of life I'm going into as we did with the elements and the isolation, even though it was so hard at times." But I said, "I've got plans. I'm going to write about the lighthouses and our life in them."

"You're the one to do it." Elson put his arm around my shoulder, drawing me close, and said, "The time has come."

We squeezed back through the little door. I loved the pretty green of the light shining through the lens. The sun was just showing above the horizon. I snapped the switch to "off" and watched the wires in the big bulb turn from red to black. I reached for the linen lens cover Elson was holding out to me and wrapped it around the lens like a mother wrapping her baby in its blanket. As I rubbed the chamois a few times over the brass, a last tribute to a shining friend, I found myself filled with many emotions.

Turning to Elson, I said, "Today, you get a special breakfast."

"I'll be along in a few minutes." He too was filled with emotion.

Never in my dreams as a child and young person did I ever think I would be a lighthouse keeper's wife and live in lighthouses for twenty-eight years. Now, I never see a light shining from these beacons but I am filled with a sense of peace and security, a sense of the trust that has gladdened the hearts of sailors all over the world for more than two thousand years.

As I began to think of how it all started my mind trailed back to the beginning of the beginnings for us.

S O U T H   L U B E C

It was a beautiful morning that July day in 1918, and I decided to go up to the creek a short distance from our home in South Lubec, Maine, to pick some goose tongue greens. I left my shoes on the bank and waded out to the grassy mounds nesting in black muck. As the tide ebbed, the mounds would be little islands. Here the eelgrass grew and in the eelgrass I would find the greens. Some were about a foot long and some, growing among the rocks, were shorter. Covered with freckles, they must resemble a goose's tongue to have been given such a name. Having the salty taste of the ocean, they were good cooked with sweet salt pork. Today I was picking them to break raw into our salads, though if we ate too many raw our cheeks would feel puckered.

My bare feet moved carefully in the sharp-edged eelgrass. It was so peaceful. The sky was azure blue with a few floating, white, feathery clouds. A gull dipped low over my head hoping I would share something with him. As I stepped into the water, I could feel tiny minnows swimming over my feet.

My basket was almost filled when I heard my brother Gerald calling me. He was two and a half years younger than I, but we were inseparable. Gerald loved the creek and we spent many hours playing there. He would gather pieces of boards he found on the beach and pretend to build a sardine factory (sardine packing was the chief industry in Lubec), while I would gather the largest peas I could find in the garden. We would remove the peas from the pods and eat them for lunch; then we'd break toothpicks into small pieces to place in the middle and at the ends of each pod to act as thwarts. We'd sail our peapod boats in the shallow water of the creek and fill them with the tiny minnows which we took back to the sardine factory to pack for sardines. Mother said she always knew where to find us.

I had four brothers and sisters. Carleton, eight years younger than I, was only nine. Of the older children, Gerald was the student in the family; my sister Minnie, the milliner and seamstress; my sister Alice, the musician. At seventeen, I tried to be a little of each, but my great desire was to be a portrait painter or a writer. Unfortunately, there was no opportunity for me to learn either of these arts. Besides, neither was considered a vocation, but rather a waste of time. I could only wish.

This day it didn't seem to matter that I was not given the talents my brother and sisters had. I wondered about many things as I stood in the marsh in the soft summer breeze. Whoever found that these greens were good to eat? Who named them? What caused the tides? Where did all the water go when it ebbed to leave these flats and marshes dry, then returned in six hours deep enough to float a large boat at the very spot in which I was standing?

My thoughts were interrupted as Gerald called again.

Wondering why he was so anxious for me to come ashore, I waded towards the bank to a shallow pool of clear salt water. I washed the muck from my feet, drying them with the towel I had brought along for that purpose. Gerald waited on the bank.

"Dad is home. He's brought a guest and Mother needs you," said Gerald, taking my basket.

The highway was just a dirt road as paving hadn't reached our area. We had had a long spell of dry weather, and when a car went by it would raise a cloud from the two inches of powdery dust covering the road. The thick dust felt good on our bare feet.

Gerald stood watching me and said: "You know, Connie, Mother would not approve of this, especially a girl of your age."

"I know, but it is fun, isn't it?" I replied. I knew what he meant: Mother was very aristocratic and tried to raise us up dignified.

A small brook ran beside the road just before the house. It was nearly dried up, but enough water remained for us to wash our feet before we went into the house. When I opened the back door I was glad to see that the door to the kitchen was closed. I went up the back stairs to my room to freshen up to meet the guest Dad had brought home.

When I went down to the kitchen, which smelled of baked chicken and dressing, I was greeted by Mother. "It's time you're home, Constance. (Mother always called me Constance, never Connie.) I've got to go to the ship launching in Dennysville and I'm in a hurry."

Mother was a small woman. I looked at her, thinking how pretty she was with her flushed face and the little damp curl that had escaped to her forehead. As she set the table, I noticed how lovely her hands were. To look at her you would never know she had worked all morning preparing the dinner and doing all the chores necessary to keep her family and house neat and clean. I couldn't ever remember seeing my mother untidy.

She had all the responsibility of bringing up us children as Dad was gone most of the time. He was one of the original crew at the lifesaving station at Quoddy Head and served a total of thirty years, becoming a member of the Coast Guard when it took over the Lifesaving Service in 1915.

Dad was home one day in seven. When we were children Mother would say, "Your father is coming home today," and we were scrubbed, our hair washed and combed, our best clothes put on us. We would sit out on the front porch and watch for Dad to appear at the top of Creath's Hill. When we happily ran to meet him, he would greet us with a smile and a hug. He was very special to us, and he made us feel very special too. He always had something in his pocket for us. Once a box under his arm contained a baby raccoon; its mother had been killed, so he brought it home for us to take care of.

One day we hurried to meet him, but when we were nearly to him, Gerald stopped short and, using the term we used for Dad at that time, said, "That is not my Papa!" We started to run back home. Then Papa called to us. I recognized his voice and stopped. Even though it did not look like Papa, I could not forget his voice, with its mixture of sternness, love, and fun. I was mystified.

This man was clean-shaven. Papa wore a mustache. He had lost his hair when he was very young, which left him quite bald except for a few hairs he would comb and comb; I wondered if he could even see them. The mustache made him handsome. I usually didn't like beards and mustaches, but on Papa the mustache was perfect.

It seemed that Mother wanted him to shave it off, so, to please her, he had done so, though he liked it because it hid what he thought was his long upper lip.

All that day Gerald would not accept him as his Papa, so it was agreed that Papa had to grow back the mustache to make him handsome again and reestablish him as our father. We were always careful to obey him after that for we didn't want him to shave his mustache off and be a stranger again. He would threaten to do this if we misbehaved.

I turned from watching my mother set the table and went into the pantry where the vegetables lay on the dry sink waiting for me to pare them and put them on to cook. When everything was ready, Mother took off her apron, tidied her hair, and said, "Now we can go into the living room and meet our guest."

I had wanted to rush right in the minute I got home and give Dad a big hug, for I hadn't seen him for a week. When I did enter the living room and saw him smiling at me, I rushed over and hugged him, much to the upset of my mother who did not approve of my lack of etiquette.

Dad turned to the man with him and introduced me to him. Lieutenant Lincoln took my hand and, looking at Dad, said, "It's too bad, Mr. Scovill, that you have to be away from your family for such long periods. I'm glad to be a part of a family who care so much."

I looked over to my mother and she was smiling.

Lieutenant Lincoln was the officer sent to the Coast Guard stations to inspect them. He was a long way from home, so Dad had invited him to dinner and to go to the launching of a vessel at Dennysville.

Mother's dinner was delicious as always. I knew Dad was proud of her. Besides all the work she did in the house and with the family, she had a sweet soprano voice and sang in the church choir. Every Saturday night she had the choir at our house to practice for the next day's service. She also was asked to sing at all the funerals.

We went to the launching in Lieutenant Lincoln's car, as we didn't own one then. We had passed the standpipe at the ridge when we met a car that slowed down, the people in it waving to us. Both cars stopped because Dad recognized Captain Fred Small and his family. They were coming to visit Mother and Dad, and Dad wanted to go back home to visit. But the Smalls wouldn't hear of it and decided to join us for the launching. In the car were Captain Fred Small and his wife, his parents, and his son. Captain Bert, Fred Small's father, got out of the car followed by the young man, who was in uniform, and came to my side of the car where he introduced me to his grandson, Elson. Captain Bert was very eager that we meet, but Elson wasn't eager at all.

I had known Captain Bert for a long time, since I was twelve, and I'd met him when I visited my sister Minnie with her family at Avery Rock Lighthouse in Machias Bay near Captain Bert's home. After he retired from the sea, he'd served in the Maine legislature. When he retired from the legislature he took a job as lobster warden from Quoddy Head to Jonesport and stayed at our home whenever he was in our area. I didn't know that he had made up his mind to make a match between Elson and me and that was why he was anxious for us to meet.

Captain Bert knew that my family, like Elson's, was born to the sea. He had owned his own vessels and sailed to the West Indies and South America. How I wished I could take short-hand when we sat and listened to him tell his sea stories. I first learned that there was an eye in a hurricane when I heard him tell Elson, "*Si*, Elson, we were running from South America to Boston with a load of salt when a hurricane caught up with us. I was trying to reach the eye of the hurricane where I could lay out the storm, but the vessel was pounded so hard by the waves she opened at the seams and she sank beneath us. We managed to get away in the lifeboat and survived until we were rescued."

He told of the time he'd been to Barbados for a load of molasses when a hurricane overtook the ship. "*Si*, Elson, that was a bad one. I was at the helm, the mate directing the crew, when a huge wave came, washing the mate and sailors the length of the deck. The mate was just being washed over the rail when I grabbed him by his oilskin and held him until he could get his sealegs firmly on the deck. The sailors were not as fortunate, as we never saw some of them again. The sails were blown away and we wallowed in the sea until it was over and we finally got back to port."

Captain Bert was only one of many members of Elson's family to follow the sea. Elson's father was a warrant officer in the Coast Guard all his life. Elson's Uncle Clair and his mother's father were both sea captains. His Uncle Garfield was a mate.

My family followed the sea also. My Grandfather Myers was a sea captain and my great-great-grandfather owned and sailed ships. Uncle Loring Myers retired as a shipmaster in 1890. He made his first trip to sea at the age of nine in about 1864. He became keeper at Channel Light near Lubec and would retire from there in 1923. Also an inventor, he patented a number of inventions including an unsinkable lifeboat. Two brothers of my mother's were lost at sea together, the younger on his first voyage. My maternal grandmother had been a governess for the lighthouse keeper at West Quoddy Head Light; my sister Minnie married a lightkeeper and had lived at Avery Rock Light since 1913. And, of course, my father was one of the crew at the Quoddy Head Lifesaving Station.

Knowing about the sea history of my family, Captain Bert decided that his grandson and I would be a perfect match with our shared heritage. He did all he could to make this match happen.

Elson Leroy Small was tall and blond and had a military stance in his uniform. Despite his austere manner, I saw that he acknowledged the introduction with a smile and a twinkle in his blue eyes.

We continued on to Dennysville. When we reached the launching spot we met some more friends, these from Bucks Harbor. One was a girl who was very interested in Elson and they strolled off together, much to the disappointment of Captain Bert. I didn't see Elson again until we were leaving.

Gerald and I had a grand time watching the big vessel slide down the ways, and the wake she made christening her hull. Before we left, Elson's grandmother invited me to come for a visit. I had visited with Elson's grandparents and Aunt Ethel, who lived with them and ran the house, many times, so I promised I'd come when I could. A few weeks after the launching, Mother and Father decided to go to Bucks Harbor to visit my sister Minnie. I went with them for a long visit with the Smalls.

Elson's grandparents and aunt had just finished greeting us when Elson appeared, much to his grandfather's delight. After my folks left he remained. His cousin Elton came in, so the conversation was lively and interesting, for both Elton and his wife were teachers and kept up with all the current events, local and national.

After Elton left, I was surprised to hear Elson ask, "What time are you having supper, Aunt Ethel?"

"The same as usual, five o'clock."

"OK, I'll be back." Turning to me, he said, "I have to see Percy Colbeth. Would you like to take a walk with me to the beach where Percy is working on his boat?"

I looked up at Elson's grandmother who was teaching me to crochet a very pretty lace pattern, but she said we could finish it the next day.

We walked down the road to Percy's house, then followed the path beside the house to the shore. Percy was aboard his boat, tied to the mooring, but when Elson called to him he started for shore in the dinghy. As he neared the beach he folded the oars on the thwarts, jumped over the side into water nearly to the top of his rubber hip boots, and waded to shore, guiding his boat onto the beach.

"Hello, Elson, my boy. Glad to see you. You home to stay?"

"Just for a couple of weeks until I join the *Lake Shawano* in Boston."

Percy then turned to me, saying, "Hi there. Have you been homesick lately?"

I already knew Percy. I had met his stepdaughter, Beulah, when I was twelve and was visiting my sister at Avery Rock. On one trip ashore I met Beulah, who invited me to visit her, so I went in from Avery Rock to spend the weekend. It was a weekend I'll never forget.

I was a shy, quiet, frightened child, who was also quite obedient. I feared I'd do something wrong and people wouldn't like me. Beulah was just the opposite. She played tricks on me and did little things that I was afraid her mother wouldn't like. They weren't bad things, but what I thought we shouldn't do.

The house Beulah lived in with her grandmother was Cape Cod style with stairs between the parlor and the living room, leading up to the second floor where there was a bedroom on each side of the stairs. The kitchen was in an ell on the first floor with a bedroom above where Beulah's grandmother slept. We had one of the rooms in the main part of the house; it seemed a long way from her grandmother. Beulah thought she would have fun with me, so she told me I would have to crawl through a long passageway full of bats to get to the bathroom. I was just stupid enough to believe her and didn't sleep all night, fearing the bats would come out and land on us.

By morning I was thinking how good it would be if I could walk home. However, we had fun that day and Beulah seemed to forget about trying to scare me. But as it got toward late afternoon I was feeling pretty homesick and asked Beulah if she would take me over to her mother's house so I could ask Percy to row me out to Avery Rock. I wanted so badly to get there I didn't even think about whether it might be too rough to land on the Rock.

Percy hadn't arrived back from hauling his lobster traps, but Mrs. Colbeth thought he would be home soon. All this time Beulah was coaxing me to go back with her. Soon Percy came, hungry and tired, with cows waiting for him to milk, but when he saw how badly I was feeling, he said, "I'll row you out and if it's too rough to land, we'll take care of you."

We bounced up and down on the waves as he rowed the two miles or more over the choppy sea. When we finally reached the Rock, I couldn't wait to jump ashore as soon as I saw the smiling faces of my family. Percy wouldn't stay for supper, nor would he take any pay for his time. He was a real friend in need.

Before the summer was over I had a chance to think over this visit and decided I had been a very ungrateful girl, for these people were so kind and, after all, Beulah was just having fun. Later in the summer I went in and stayed a couple of days with her. We laughed about the bats and how silly I was to believe such a thing. We became good friends after that, and I visited her many times, but I had learned that it isn't any fun to be home-sick!

This visit was what Percy meant when he greeted me. Elson had quite a laugh when we told him about it. I don't think I ever lived it down.

We had come to see Percy to get lobsters, so we rowed out with him to his lobster pound and Elson selected several large ones. When we returned to his grandmother's, Elson and his Aunt Ethel took them out to the little shop in back of the house where there was a stove used for cooking lobsters, wild duck, or coots that had a strong odor that would smell up the house.

Elson's Aunt Ethel was a meticulous housekeeper. There was never a speck of dust or a thing out of place in her home. The house was large: five bedrooms, sewing room, parlor, living room, dining room, kitchen like a family room, pantry, and back hall. All was furnished and polished to the umpth degree. Most of the family said they didn't like to go beyond the kitchen for fear they would disturb something; only Elson seemed totally comfortable here.

Aunt Ethel gave me one of her best bedrooms to sleep in. Dainty rosebud paper covered the walls; lace curtains hung at the window; a brass and white enamel, iron bedstead and a bureau and commode of bird's-eye maple furnished the room. Braided rugs on the floor, a chair with needlepoint on the back and seat, and a bureau scarf of embroidered flowers all were the work of Aunt Ethel's hands. It was a lovely room. I knelt to say thank you.

I got to know Elson during my stay. Besides being tall, blond, and blue-eyed, he was very agile and a tease, with a lively attitude. He had a nice tenor voice and played a number of musical instruments. Girls all liked him. One in particular kept asking him to her house to play his banjo, guitar, accordion, mandolin, or harmonica, while she accompanied him on the organ.

Every morning Elson came to his aunt's house. We took walks on the shore, and he'd take Percy's boat and row me around the harbor. He introduced me to all of his family and took me to meet his special friends. He told me I had lovely eyes. We had a wonderful two weeks. Then my visit was up, and I was leaving for home in two days; he was going to Boston to join the ship sailing for Cuba on which he was third officer.

The day before he was to leave for Boston he was so busy I didn't see him until evening. When he came he was not the happy, teasing person he had been, but was very serious. We sat long after the family had gone to bed at nine o'clock. At first we both sat quietly. It had been a nice, friendly two weeks, and I knew I was going to miss his companionship. I was also concerned about one so young taking so much responsibility. He was twenty-one. He had graduated from navigation school with a third mate's license, unlimited, and a pilot's license from Boston to Gay Head, Massachusetts.

He sat at one end of the table, I was at the other. He looked up and said, "I didn't sleep much last night, as I did a lot of thinking. I was wondering about choosing the sea. I had wanted to be a doctor. Every time Dr. Larson came with his little black bag I decided I wanted to follow in his footsteps, helping sick people. But I also had a dream of being the best captain of the largest ship afloat. I've been on vessels since I was fourteen years old — one summer on the cup racer, another on a seagoing yacht. The sea won, the feeling of the salty spray it and the challenge of a ship against the waves."

He paused and looking at me, said, "Do you think my decision was right?"

The question surprised me. I didn't know what to answer. Finally I replied, "I can see that the pull of the sea is greater than the land. I guess you'll have to make this trip on the steamer to settle it in your mind."

He seemed to relax. Glancing at the clock, he said, "Goodness gracious, it's late. The folks will be wondering. I must leave." Coming around the table, he took my hand and drew me to my feet, saying, "This has been a nice two weeks and I hate to go. As soon as I get my new address, will you write to me?" Then he surprised me by kissing me, and was gone.

A bit dazed, I stood in front of the closed door. I turned away thinking I'd probably never see him again, but it was only a few days after I returned home that I got a letter asking again if I would write to him.

In this first letter he wrote, "I haven't much time to write for we are sailing tomorrow. We're going coastwise as there are a lot of German submarines out there. Thank you for helping me when you said I'd have to make this trip to decide whether I'd still want the sea."

Whenever his ship came to Boston to load or unload, Elson took the train in Boston at night, arriving in Eastport the next morning. He would appear at my parents' home in Lubec even though it might be for just overnight, although usually we had several days. He would come in, grab me around the waist, and waltz me around. As Mother said, "He's like a fresh breeze." He seemed to fit in with the family, and I began to watch for the surprise visits and for his letters.

A year slipped by. I hadn't seen Elson for three months when his ship came to Searsport on the Penobscot River to unload. We had little time together this trip because transportation between Searsport and Lubec was so difficult and time-consuming. To get back to the ship, Elson had to hire a car and driver to take him to Machias in order to get a train to Bangor. He asked me to go with him to Machias.

It was a nice summer day, but I don't think either one of us cared as we were so happy to be with each other. We were sitting close together in the back seat when he said softly, "I came to ask you if you would spend your life with me, even though we won't see much of each other. I'll be at sea for long periods of time."

From his pocket he took out a small, blue box. When he opened it there was a lovely diamond. He put it on my finger, and somewhere between Lubec and Machias we sealed our betrothal with a kiss.

It wasn't until I returned home and showed Mother and Father my ring that I realized I was an engaged lady. I began to think of what it meant and whether I really was ready for it. I had pledged myself to a man I would see six or eight times during the year.

When I was deeply disturbed about something I'd go into the parlor and play my favorite songs on the piano or go to my room and draw or read poems. Then my soul would be calmed. I did these things often during this time.

When my friends heard about the diamond they came to see it and to give me a lot of advice. With their interest, I became happier and more hopeful.

My sister Minnie's husband, Charlie, was still stationed as keeper at Avery Rock Lighthouse. Minnie came home for a visit and asked me to go back with her when she returned.

Avery Rock consisted of a large rock and a smaller one. When the tide was high, twelve feet of water flowed between the rocks, but when it was low the two rocks were one. A bridge over what we called the gulch connected the two. The oil house, supply building, outdoor bathroom (very inconvenient when it stormed or was very cold in the winter), house, and bell tower were on the larger rock, the boat house on the smaller one.

We reached the Rock on one of those rare summer days when the sea was calm and there was no undertow. Minnie and Charlie were the parents of four children aged twelve, ten, six, and five. Beulah, the oldest, was a trustworthy child and very capable, both with the other children and in helping around the lighthouse. When Charlie took the powerboat to Bucks Harbor to pick us up, he had given instructions to Beulah to keep the children away from the water and not let them near the edge of the rocks.

The sail around the islands and across the bay was beautiful. It was so good to be with Minnie and Charlie again. Since Minnie was almost sixteen years older than I and had taken care of me when I was little, she seemed more like a mother to me than a sister. We were very close. Charlie was like a brother as he had been with the family as long as I could remember.

Charlie was tying the boat to the mooring when Minnie, who had been watching the children line up like stair steps at the boat house door, became frantic, ready to swim ashore. She saw that the smallest one was not there. Charlie got us ashore in record time. Both speaking at the same time, they asked Beulah where Crawford was.

"He's sleeping, Mother," she said.

We all relaxed and walked slowly to the house enjoying the scenery. We had just reached the door when a trembling, crying Beulah put her arms around her mother saying, "I did everything I remembered. Please don't be angry with me." She sobbed in her mother's embrace.

Then she said, "Daddy, there was no boats passing and besides I had no time to semaphore for help." When Beulah was eight she had learned the semaphore and would signal the Navy and Coast Guard boats and the lighthouse tender and talk with them.

When the sobs subsided, Minnie and I followed her into the kitchen where Crawford was lying on the couch, wrapped in blankets and sleeping peacefully. Then the story came out, Ira and Viola both talking excitedly at once.

Crawford had gotten away from Beulah, and thinking a piece of driftwood was his boat, reached too far and fell into the twelve-foot water of the gulch between the two rocks. Beulah ran after him, grabbing a gaff that her father used to hook the lobster traps. When she got to the water, Crawford was coming up for the first time. It was his second time up before she was able to catch his clothes in the hook. She pulled him ashore, rolled out the water, and carried him to the house where she wrapped him in blankets and he fell asleep. No lifesaver could have done better. We all tried to make Beulah realize that.

I was shaking all over and went out and walked

around the cement patio. I looked out over the small pile of rock thinking what a place it was for anyone to live, especially anyone with small children. Little did I realize that four years later I would be living on this same pile of rock.

My being at Avery Rock with my sister gave her a break since I could stay and tend the light and she could go with Charlie to visit friends and have a change from the isolation. Ordinarily one or the other had to stay on the Rock.

During my visit I went ashore to visit Elson's sister. I had known Evelyn for several years and had visited her often, but had never met Elson as he was away all the time. Also, I had had no interest in him. Now Evelyn was going to be married that summer and I was engaged, so we had lots to talk about.

Her hope chest interested me very much. She had had a box made from pine and had covered it with a beautiful, rose print cretonne. Then she had padded and tufted it with large gold-headed studs which I thought made it very pretty. The chest was filled with linens of all kinds, some trimmed with lace, some hemstitched, and some with knitted lace; all were very lovely. I hoped I could have a chest like it.

Evelyn was delighted that Elson and I were engaged. She talked about him, about how he loved to play the banjo and mandolin, to sing and laugh. She said he was a tease and she often would get mad at him.

Evelyn and I had good times together. Her father was captain at the Coast Guard station on Cross Island and we kept house when her mother went to visit him. Evelyn would make fudge, going to the milk room and skimming the golden cream from the top of the milk so the fudge made with it melted in your mouth. My family either made cream into butter or sold it, so I was quite concerned about her skimming the cream, but she assured me it was okay.

Once, Evelyn's mother phoned that she and the captain were coming over to the mainland for the day and Evelyn should make a beef stew, giving her instructions on how to make it. One of the ingredients was a half-cup of rice. Evelyn put that into the stew. Thinking it was not enough as we could hardly see it, she added another cup. This didn't look like enough either, so she added another cup. As the stew cooked, the rice began to come over the top of the kettle so fast it took the two of us to stop it and to clean the stove. The folks never did get that stew.

I had been back on the Rock a few days when I saw a rowboat coming around the weir at Bear Island. I just knew it was Elson on one of his surprise visits. He had written me that he had his second mate's license and was on a ship sailing from New York to Rotterdam. Charlie brought the spyglasses when I called to him, and sure enough, it was Elson.

He looked so handsome with his two gold stripes and a new cap with a shining gold band and insignia. In two more years, at only twenty-six, he would be the captain he wanted to be. We sat on a big boulder as he told me about the trip he had just made to Holland and gave me the souvenirs he had brought. I was so proud of him. Soon, however, he said, "I have something I must ask you."

The war was over and the bottom was dropping out of the Merchant Marine. It had been decided that the captains and the mates would go on the active ships for six months, then come ashore and let other captains and mates have their turn.

"When we came in to Boston this trip, I met Captain Carl Sherman who is superintendent of the First Lighthouse District," said Elson. "He asked me if I would consider taking a position as assistant keeper of a lighthouse that would soon be vacated. I can stay until shipping picks up again, and when our family comes along, I'll go back to sea."

He looked intently into my eyes. I realized what he was going to ask me. "Do you love me enough to go with me on a lighthouse?"

The world I had pictured living in contained a nice home surrounded with lots of flowers, a family, and a place in the community. These dreams, as well as my dream of making a home my husband would love to relax in and rest from the rugged sea, were collapsing. Hadn't I thought a few days ago that a place like Avery Rock was no place for anyone to live?

I felt Elson looking at me, understanding the feelings of a nineteen-year-old. When I looked up and saw his love shining out to me, I knew that I had to say yes.

PHOTOGRAPHS

I. Mabel Myers Scovill (1867-1957), Connie's mother, shortly after her marriage. Photograph *circa* 1885.

II. Ira Elroy Scovill (1864-1930), Connie's father, West Quoddy Head, *circa* 1915.

III. Connie and her brother Gerald, South Lubec, *circa* 1908.

IV. Lifesaving Station Crew, Quoddy Head, (Connie's father in center), *circa* 1907.

V. Captain Fred Small with daughter Evelyn and son Elson, Cross Island Coast Guard Station, *circa* 1905.

VI. Constance Scovill, sixteen years old, 1917.

VII. Connie at Elson's Aunt Ethel's home, Bucks Harbor, *circa* 1918.

VIII. Elson and Connie on Avery Rock, on the day Elson "proposed the lighthouse life," 1920.

IX. Mary Jane Bleumortier Myers (1834-1928), Connie's grandmother, South Lubec, *circa* 1906.

X. Connie and Elson, July 1921, eight months after their wedding.

XI. Channel Light, Lubec, 1920.

XII. Connie (waving) and her cousin, Emma Davis, Channel Light, Lubec, 1921.

XIII. Connie (left) and her cousin, Emma Davis, Channel Light, Lubec, 1921.

XIV. Connie and Elson, with neighbor children, Lubec, 1921.

XV. Avery Rock Light Station, Machias Bay, 1922.

XVI. Elson's sister, Evelyn, in the gulch, Avery Rock Light Station, 1923.

XVII. Connie "all dressed up; no place to go," Avery Rock Light Station, 1923.

XVIII. Elson attaches line to *Dream* on the slip at Avery Rock Light Station, *circa* 1923.

XIX. Connie and Elson's furniture on Seguin tramway (144 ft. elevation), *circa* 1930.

XX. Seguin Light Station, Kennebec River, 1898.

XXI. Dwellings and light on Seguin, 1898.

XXII. Tramway (far left), boathouse, light, and keeper's house, Seguin, 1898.
Beneath is beach where Connie found coal.

XXIII. Saint Croix River Light, Dochet's Island, and keeper's house, *circa* 1935.

XXIV. Elson and Connie on Dochet's Island with FDR's Christmas tree, December 9, 1941.

XXV. Elson and ice at Dochet's Island, March 1931.

XXVI. Connie and ice at Dochet's Island, March 1931.

XXVII. Saint Croix River Light, Dochet's Island, 1930.

XXVIII. Elson on Dochet's Island, 1941.

XXIX. Elson with cow (nationally circulated Coast Guard photograph), Dochet's Island, 1945.

XXX. Elson (behind wheel) and friend from Red Beach on home-made raft, 1941.

XXXI. Connie and Elson at Portsmouth Harbor Light, New Castle, New Hampshire, 1946.
Keeper's home in background.

XXXII. Elson and Connie, Portsmouth Harbor Light, New Castle, 1946.

XXXIII. Elson in motorboat, Portsmouth Harbor Light in background, *circa* 1947.

XXXIV. Connie and Elson's home in Eliot, Maine, 1948.

XXXV. "Mother Small," Connie as a Head Resident at University of Maine at Farmington, 1964.

XXXVI. Connie Scovill Small, 1998.
(Photograph copyright 1998 by Frank Clarkson.)

C H A N N E L   L I G H T

Grandmother Myers was a wise and caring person we grandchildren felt we could confide in; she was the one we went to with our troubles. When I had ended my visit to Avery Rock and returned home, I decided to talk with her. Whenever she saw any of us coming, Grandmother would put the teakettle on and bring out the milk crackers she kept to treat us. When I was in high school I would stop on the way home for tea and the crackers and a visit with her. These crackers, now called Royal Lunch crackers, are still my favorites.

I walked the three miles to her home overlooking Passamaquoddy Bay. Grandmother didn't see me coming. Absorbed in thought, she sat in her favorite chair, stroking a purring kitten as she looked out over the bay toward Channel Light, watching for her son, my Uncle Loring Myers, to row back to his house next door on his days off the light. When I arrived she started to rise, but I said, "Don't get up, Grandmother. I just want to talk with you."

"Now, my dear, we can talk much better over a cup of

tea. You put the teakettle on and I'll get the crackers." Grandmother was eighty-nine years old. A bit on the plump side, but tall and stately, she looked twenty years younger. We never thought of her as being old.

She poured the boiling water over the tea leaves she'd put in the teapot, and said, as always, "It has to brew a few minutes to be good." I helped her get the china cups she used for tea and poured the milk into the tiny pitcher. The crackers took on the appearance of a special treat as she arranged them on a plate with hand-painted roses. She returned to her chair, placing her cup and saucer on the table beside her, making a space for mine. I sat on the stool next to her and felt a great peace and closeness, as though I belonged just to her.

"How come serving tea is so important to you and Mother?" I asked. "Are you French, or English?"

She looked at me thoughtfully. "I think you're worrying about living in a lighthouse, and its isolation. If you can delay your talk for a while, I'll tell you the history of our family. It may help you to understand what true love and sacrifice can be. When you feel that life as the wife of a lighthouse keeper is lonely and dull and full of sacrifices, it may help you to endure."

She settled back in her chair and rocked back and forth for a few moments. Then she began, "My grandmother was a French baroness, Sophia de Raddecliffe. Her family's estate was near the king's palace. She was betrothed to a nobleman, but she had no intention of marrying him for she had fallen in love with a young man whose father was captain of the king's wine cellar. However, they could not marry in France since she was of the nobility and he a commoner. The only way they could marry was to elope to Sweden, which meant she would have to give up her title, her family, and her home."

"Oh, Grandmother! Wasn't there any way at all except for her to lose her family?" I said.

"No, my dear, she was faced with being cut off. So, they eloped to Sweden and there my father was born in Stockholm, where he was educated and studied to be a cabinetmaker. When he graduated he was given five hundred dollars and a set of tools, and he set sail for the new country of America to start a business. But this was at the time of the French and English war; the ship was captured, he was thrown into the dungeon of the prison at Louisbourg on Cape Breton.

"He and another man dug their way out, found a boat, and started for Boston. But in a heavy gale they were wrecked on Grand Manan Island in the Bay of Fundy. He settled there, married Mary Wormell, and raised a family of children and grandchildren. It was on Grand Manan that I was born. I grew up and wanted to live in the states, so when the chance came for me to be governess to the children of the lighthouse keeper at West Quoddy Head Lighthouse, I took it. I met your grandfather and came as a bride to this house.

"I have lived in a lighthouse and know its loneliness. When you get discouraged and lonely, think of Sophia and the sacrifices she made, the loneliness she must have felt in that strange country. Perhaps her experience will sustain you."

"You've answered my question, Grandmother." I said. "You knew all along what was worrying me."

I left Grandmother's and walked down to her beach. Out in the bay, Channel Light's familiar cylinder shape rose starkly out of the water. My uncle was head keeper. I walked slowly along the beach, kicking stones and leaning down to draw pictures in the wet sand. Then I realized I was drawing lighthouses.

There was a fight inside me. I wanted to live where there were people and houses and flowers and a chance to learn how to paint and write. If I were a captain's wife, I would live where his ship was based, maybe near Boston or New York. I would be near schools where I could learn.

I stubbed my toe and fell on the sand. The toe hurt so badly I wanted to cry. Just then a small steamer passing the lighthouse blew three blasts of her whistle, and soon the bell answered with three sweet tones. The sound entered my soul and stayed there. No longer did I wallow in self-pity, but instead wondered at how nice it was to have a man who loved me enough to spend a life with me away from all he no doubt wanted to do.

I forgot my hurt and hurried up the bank. I quickly walked the three miles home, now and then waving to neighbors along the way. I was eager to write Elson to tell him I hoped he'd get home soon.

A letter from him was waiting at the house. Hurrying upstairs to read it, I hugged it unopened to me for a few moments, wondering where our course would take us.

Elson started the letter by telling me about his trip to Holland and the eight-year-old girl who lived on a barge near where the ship was docked. He'd taken a great liking to her, and one of the crew acted as interpreter when they talked. Then he wrote, "The day we sailed I got my papers saying I'd been assigned to Lubec Channel Light Station to take effect November first, 1920. The ship is due in Boston October first. I'll be packing my seabag and heading for Bucks Harbor and to you as soon after as possible. We can start making our plans."

It was official! I was going to be a lightkeeper's wife. How strange his assignment should be to the very lighthouse whose sweet bell tones had entered my soul and stayed. I was beginning to feel excited. Life in a lighthouse would be an adventure. I'd learn about the sea and its hazards and be a part of helping to guide sailors. I could hardly wait for Elson to come home!

Elson began his duties at Channel Light on November 1, 1920, and we were married on November 23. The winter before, I'd been very sick with pneumonia which had progressed into severe asthma, therefore I didn't dare plan the church wedding I'd always wanted. We decided to have a very quiet ceremony and were to be married in the parsonage of the Christian Church in Lubec, with the Reverend C. D. Nutter performing the ceremony.

The day of our wedding, Elson and I left my parents' house in snow, a wind blowing hard from the northeast. On the way to the church, Elson went down to the shore and hauled his boat on the bank, covering it to secure it as the sea was rough and the surf running high. My father was sick, and my mother stayed home with him, but my sister Alice and her husband, Clarence Ramsdell, and my brother Gerald were to be our attendants. Elson had hired Roland Libby to drive us in his horse drawn sleigh the three miles to the village. By the time we reached the parsonage Reverend Nutter had received a call from Alice saying the storm was so bad they couldn't get through the drifts, so Mrs. Nutter, Gerald, and Roland were our attendants.

I proudly wore a blue velour suit with a white lace blouse and blue velvet hat. I suspected I was going to have an asthma attack when I began to have trouble breathing as I removed my coat and overshoes, but I did my best to hide it. However, when we were leaving the parsonage, Elson noticed my difficulty and helped me with my overshoes and wrapped my scarf tightly around my neck to keep out the snow: one of so many little kindnesses he did in our life together which lasted forty years lacking one day.

There were no snowplows in those days, and we had quite a hard time getting home. The drifts were very deep, so the men walked and led the horse through the snow which was still coming down hard. By the time we got to my parents' house I was really gasping for breath. Doctor Bennett was called; he came on foot, leading his horse, and had to stay all night until the road crew could break through the drifts with hand shovels and then drive a big sled through to make a road.

The asthma attack had made me terribly nervous and scared. I was sorry for Elson who sat on one side of the bed holding my hand, while Doctor Bennett sat holding my other hand. Hoping to relieve the tension, I said, between gasps, "This is some wedding night."

They responded, but I could see that Doctor Bennett was holding something back. Finally he said, "I've been treating you since last March and every attack gets worse. The only things I can give you are morphine or adrenaline but I can't do that any longer or you'll get to depend on them."

Just then the part-collie, part-shepherd dog I loved so much came to the door to see what was happening to me, and Elson spoke up, "I think it's the dog that's causing this."

Doctor Bennett didn't agree with him, but simply said, "You must not stay here or come here anymore. There is something here that is causing this asthma and you cannot live with it."

I could not conceive of not being able to come home to visit my mother and father whom I loved so dearly. I remembered so many instances of their caring for me.

Just that year when I'd been so ill with pneumonia I would become conscious of them standing over me in the dining room, which was my sickroom, dressed in their outer winter clothing, testing the temperature of the bricks they'd heated and placed down my sides. It was a cold January day, but the window had been taken out and the space covered with cheesecloth to keep out the snow while giving me all the air possible. The room was freezing as they cooled my burning lips with water, and whispered encouragement.

With this memory and so many others, I hated the thought of not being able to come into their house again. But, faced with the doctor's orders to leave the house as soon as possible, we moved to our rent in South Lubec before it was ready for us. In a week's time I was over the asthma and had some of my strength back.

I shall never forget how badly my father felt when I left his home. Fortunately we were only a quarter of a mile away, so he would come to visit us every day, or I would walk down to his house and sit on the porch and visit, never tiring of the view across Passamaquoddy Bay, Quoddy Head, and the Bay of Fundy. He talked of his memories of his duty in the crew at Quoddy Head Lifesaving Station. In fact, he finally retired after thirty years because of injuries he'd received as part of that crew.

I remembered that winter day when I was a child, when he and the crew went to a vessel in trouble on the rocks off Quoddy Head. The temperature was twenty-two degrees below zero, the vapor so thick the vessel and the lifesaving crew could not be seen from shore. Several days passed with no word; the wives were frantic, fearing that their husbands had been lost. Finally, the men returned, but my father had frozen his foot by standing hour after hour on an iron winch, forgetting his discomfort as he did his job of saving the vessel and its crew. Father was brought home to recover, and Gerald and I would creep up the stairs to peek at his foot, swollen like a large balloon we were afraid would burst. Then it happened: the outer shell of his foot came off in the perfect shape of his foot and toes. The toes underneath were like the pink toes of a baby, until they gradually grew and hardened up again to a normal foot. After that he couldn't let his foot get cold or walk too far on it, so he did the cooking at the station because he couldn't do the watches over bad territory and rocks.

As Elson's wife, my relationship to Channel Light was that of a visitor. A cylinder light constructed of iron and steel, situated in the channel that divides Lubec in Maine and Campobello Island in New Brunswick, Canada, Channel Light was a two-man stag light. Wives and families of the keepers didn't live on it. My Uncle Low, Captain Loring Myers, was head keeper and Elson his first assistant. Their schedule was two days on duty, two days ashore, and since my uncle was head keeper I could go out and be with Elson once in a while when he was on duty, though I lived in our rent at South Lubec.

The first time I went out to the light with Elson to stay two days, it was nearly winter. The morning was beautiful, the air cool as we walked briskly up the beach from my grandmother's house to the sandy rock bar that extended nearly to the lighthouse from Lubec Point. It was almost low tide and the flats were just about free of water. Uncle rowed across the narrow space of water to meet us; we then took the boat back to the light and Uncle went to his home.

We rowed to the ladder; then we had to climb to get to

the dwelling section of the light. I looked up that thirty feet of black iron and my heart went right down to my toes. I had been afraid of boats and the sea since a cousin had teasingly rocked a rowboat we were in when I was three years old. I never learned to row until after I married Elson. I was also afraid of heights, but trying not to show just how scared I was, I said to Elson, "I can never climb up there."

"Oh yes, you can. Just grab the rungs and I'll be right behind you."

So, with him behind me telling me to look up and never down, I made it. To this day I have kept his words with me and when I'd get discouraged I would think of them. They've helped me a good many times to overcome a panicky feeling and do what had to be done.

When I reached the deck I had a feeling of exultation, of succeeding, but when I went to the rail and looked down at that rushing water, I began to worry how I was ever going to get to land again. The tide by the light is very swift and strong. Passamaquoddy Bay is a large body of water. The tide rises and falls twenty-five to twenty-eight feet and passes through a very narrow channel into lower Passamaquoddy Bay, by the lighthouse and West Quoddy Head into the Bay of Fundy. All this area is the easternmost part of the United States, West Quoddy Head being the easternmost point of land. Sailrock and Gulliver's Hole, on the eastern side of Quoddy Head, are known as the graveyard of ships, and Sailrock is the easternmost piece of the United States.

We walked around the landing deck, stopping to point out my church in Lubec where we'd been married, then the yellow building where I'd gone to high school. I traced the long walk I'd had from my home in South Lubec to the high school nearly three miles away. We located the house we were now renting in South Lubec, the grade school I'd gone to as a child, and the heath we children dared to explore despite warnings that it was dangerous because it was covered with mossy vegetation that could hide a mucky hole. Once in a while we'd go onto the heath to pick a pitcher plant with its fascinating pitcher-shaped leaves and long stem topped by a dark red blossom. Next in the panorama was the Coast Guard station, which had been, until 1915, the Lifesaving Station where my father worked and where I would visit as a child to be treated to a big piece of cake he'd made. The pan was huge to my child's eyes; it had to feed a crew of seven to nine men. Elson and I continued around the deck pointing out Quoddy Head and its lighthouse, and then the entrance to the Bay of Fundy. Grand Manan Island was in the distance, and now facing us was Campobello Island.

Entering a door off the landing deck, I found myself in a cozy room. Since the light was a cylinder, all the rooms were round. The kitchen and living room were combined into the one room at this landing level. I marveled at how the cabinets, sink, and stove fit into the circular shape. I can still remember from later visits the sight of Uncle Low, in deep thought as he rocked in his favorite rocking chair by the window that looked across the water to his home in South Lubec.

The second deck was a bedroom and not nearly as cozy as the kitchen-living area. A bed, a commode, and a chair seemed to stand out in the room at odd angles. No rug was on the floor, and nothing indicated the touch of a woman's hand. It was difficult to sleep in this room; the wind whistled around the tower and pieces of driftwood hit the tower, sounding like avalanches.

Above the bedroom was the lantern deck. Channel

Light was a fifth order light, one of the least powerful lights, with a first order light being the most powerful. It had a flash every ten seconds. The lamp, which set inside the lens, was a brass hand lamp, about two and a half feet high, with a round wick which had to be trimmed with precision for it to give its maximum light and to prevent a smokeup.

Under the landing deck was the basement where rainwater caught from the roof was held in cisterns and provided the water supply for the light. Coal and oil were also stored in this basement, which was under water at medium and high tides. It was a strange sensation to go down into the basement and hear the tide flowing swiftly over your head and to hope the seams would never spring a leak. The tide flowed at the rate of eight or nine knots and as fast as fourteen to twenty at neap.

One hot summer day, Elson and I had taken our chairs out on the landing deck. The water was pale blue glass and a breeze was blowing off the land from the direction of South Lubec. We watched the gulls fly high up in the air, then fold their wings and dive for fish. A sardine boat loaded with herring for the factory at Lubec was passing, and now and then a fisherman threw out a herring or a crab and the army of gulls following staged a massive battle for the food. It was a pretty sight, the white whirling wings and yellow beaks silhouetted against the sky.

The sardine boat had just passed up the narrows when the lighthouse tender came around Quoddy Head. We hustled our chairs inside and Elson made a thorough check to make certain everything was in perfect order in case the superintendent was aboard. You never knew when your station might be inspected. We glanced over to the shore where Uncle Low lived and there he was, coming as fast as he could row, trying to make the station before the tender reached it.

I didn't want to be part of any inspection, so while the two men were busy, I went down to the basement to be out of the way. Then I realized an inspection would include the basement, and I hid in the coal bin, knowing it wouldn't be checked. I could hear the engines churning the water, getting nearer and nearer. Suddenly I feared that the tender might have come to land the coal supply and I'd be buried in the black, dusty stuff, so I put on a brave front and went up on deck.

By now the tender was abreast the light. Elson and Uncle were out on the deck. Elson rang the bell three times in salute; three white steam blasts from the tender answered. But the tender steamed right by the light, through the narrows, headed for the Saint Croix River. Large and small buoys lay on her deck, so we knew she was on buoy work, taking up buoys that had been down a long while and replacing them with freshly painted and cleaned ones.

Uncle Low was pleased that Elson had everything in order. Since it was five o'clock and he was to return to duty the next morning, Uncle decided not to row home. He told Elson to go ashore instead and stop and tell Auntie why he wouldn't return that night.

Elson had been at the light only a short time when about ten feet of the ladder rusted away. At mid and high tide the water reached the remaining ladder, but the men couldn't get on the light at low tide. To get off at low tide, they would go down the ladder as far as they could and then drop into the dory. But when I tried it, all I could see was that rushing water beneath me, and my hands refused to let go. So Elson would put me in the dory on the landing deck, where it was held by two davits, and lower me, first stern, then bow, then stern, then bow, down to the water, my hands holding onto the middle thwart for dear life. It would have taken two men working together to lower the dory on an even keel.

When Elson wanted a special dinner and I was visiting him at the light, I'd take the cooking utensils and dishes out, since there were very few there. Once, a bride of a few months, I decided to make dumplings. Elson's grandmother was an expert at dumplings, and Elson loved them. I tried to duplicate hers, making the dough from a cookbook recipe, dropping the dumplings in water I'd boiled on the black iron Atlantic coal stove, cooking them covered for twenty minutes without lifting the lid. I was very proud of myself, expecting these to be the fluffy dumplings Gram made. At the end of twenty minutes I uncovered the kettle. As I lifted the dumplings onto a plate they slid right off down back of the stove. My pride and elation vanished; dismay set in. I scooped the dumplings off the floor and saw they were like boiled leather. Evidently Elson had been watching me; I heard him laughing, but he saved my day when he said, "You've just lived up to a bride's tradition."

The rent Elson and I had in South Lubec was half of the home of Astrea Nickerson, who was living in California. We had no electricity or running water. A coal furnace heated most of our living quarters, but the kitchen was in an ell heated only by the wood stove I cooked on. On days Elson was not home, I carried the water from a spring quite a distance from the house. The clear, sweet water was worth the effort, but I had to remember to empty the water pail in the kitchen each evening when I went to bed, or I would find it frozen hard the next morning.

Elson decided to use an oil cook stove which had recently been put on the market. My father had purchased it, but it wouldn't fit in his home. This oil stove seemed ultra to me, so I decided to invite my whole family for Thanksgiving dinner. Since Elson was to be home for his two days' leave, we were quite excited. The turkey was half-cooked when the pesky burner went out, and Elson couldn't get it going again. I was in a panic; my first company meal and the family would soon be there! Elson saw I was in tears. Saying "I know your mother will help us," he took the half-done turkey under his arm and started for Mother's, a quarter of a mile down the road. Soon my brother Carleton arrived, and shortly Elson returned with my father to work on the burner, which they finally got to operate. I cooked the vegetables on the stove and everything was in order when Mother came with the turkey, saying that Alice, my next oldest sister, her husband and baby would soon arrive. Gerald came later. The dinner went off fine, but I was sure glad the dinner was the day it was; when we got up the next morning the paper we'd put on the ceiling when we moved in, and which we were so proud of, had fallen off and covered the table and the floor. What a mess!

Carleton, who was about twelve during that period, would come to stay with me often when Elson was gone, to keep me company. Once when he stayed all night, I gave him my spare room with its fluffy feather tick over the mattress. It was quite high and Carleton made a jump to get into bed. I heard a muffled hallooing, investigated, and found Carleton deep in the feather tick, scared to death. As he said after I rescued him, he thought he'd landed in a big black hole.

Carleton was always very solicitous of his family. He

would scout around for raspberries, blueberries, and other berries for Mother to preserve. After I went to housekeeping, he looked out for me. One day he sat at the side of the kitchen cabinet where I was making doughnuts, cutting them with a glass and using the top of the saltshaker to make the hole. He watched me for a while, then said, "You know, Sis, when I earn enough money, I'm going to buy you a doughnut cutter." He did and I have it to this day.

Elson had been at Channel Light two years when the keeper of Avery Rock, a Lubec boy, James Doran, asked Elson to swap positions with him as he wanted to be nearer home. Avery Rock, a one keeper family light, was at the south end of Machias Bay, near Elson's family. Elson wanted to be his own boss and figured that he could tend lobster traps for extra money. We decided to change. I didn't want to go. I knew Avery Rock only too well — but we would be together and Elson wouldn't have to travel back and forth in foul weather to be with me. As this was a mutual swap, approved but not originating in the superintendent's office, we had to find a way to move our furniture and we had to bear the expense of moving.

Elson hired a sardine boat to move us, and on October 9, 1922, we sailed out by Quoddy Head into the Bay of Fundy, one of the roughest bodies of water in the world. Passing Quoddy Light, we saluted with the boat horn and heard the bell ring in answer. This trip was my first taste of rough water. The south wind was blowing a fresh breeze; first we would be on top of a wave, then in the trough, my stomach in between. Fortunately, I did not get seasick, or perhaps our lighthouse days would have been over before they started. As the spray hit my face with its salty cold, I watched my husband in the pilothouse. He didn't appear to be feeling butterflies in his stomach like I was, nor did he appear frightened when we seemed to be headed for the bottom of the sea each time we descended a large wave. He was at home here and happy to be piloting a boat again.

No doubt the waves seemed so high and dangerous to me because, though I had lived by the sea and lived with my family's stories of it, I had little direct experience with it and feared it. I hadn't learned to swim as a child; few of us did. The water was too cold. We'd play in the shallow water of the creek when the tide was out, but when it was in and deep enough to swim, the water was icy. I hadn't been around boats much since my scare as a young child; I feared a boat would upset and dump me in the water, unable to swim. I was very timid around boats and water, unlike my two brothers, who would often be out in boats with our cousin, Jerome.

I thought of my family as we slid up and down the waves. I guess I was thinking I'd be on my own now, too far away for my mother, father, brothers and sisters to help me. My life would be very different from now on.

FOUR

AVERY ROCK

It was the tenth of October when I went on Avery Rock.
With the exception of a hurried Thanksgiving dinner
with Gram and Granpa Small, I didn't get ashore again
until the last of April. Avery Rock was the same bare
pile of rock I remembered so well from Minnie's and
Charlie's time there from 1913 until 1919. As I walked
up through the boat house to get the winch line that
first day, I looked at the snow covering everything and
thought that this was a hard time of year to begin a new
life on a bunch of rocks in the middle of nowhere. Avery
Rock was between two and a half and three miles from
the mainland, a trip that took at least forty-five minutes
to row and about twenty-five minutes in a powerboat.
And that was in good weather.

I took the winch line down the slip and hooked it to
the bow of the rowboat Elson and I had rowed over from
his grandparents' house in Bucks Harbor, where we'd
spent the night until our furniture could be landed on
the Rock. Starting back up the slip, I was careful to have

my feet firm on the cleats slippery with kelp and marine grass. I took a turn on a coil of rope to catch my breath. I still hadn't totally regained my strength from the effects of the asthma.

After Elson secured the boat we walked up the path, surveying our first home. Elson loved the sea; he also loved being home, therefore the Lighthouse Service seemed the perfect solution, and now we would finally be combining home and the sea.

Built of brick eighteen inches thick faced with boards painted white with gray trim, the house was so strongly constructed that it had to be dynamited when the station was discontinued years later. There was so little room on the rock at high tide that the light was built on top of the house. The living area had six large rooms, all floored with hard pine that shone with care.

In those days the keeper had to furnish his quarters without help from the government. We had accumulated enough furniture from Elson's relatives to furnish the spare bedroom, the dining room, the kitchen, and half the living room. My particular favorite was the Edison phonograph Aunt Ethel gave us. It used round cylinder records and featured a beautiful pink-and-gold horn decorated with hand-painted roses. Somehow it got lost when we left Seguin, our next light.

The kitchen pantry was twelve feet square, with storage and cupboards around three sides and a beautiful white sink with a red pump that brought water from the cisterns placed under a trapdoor expertly hidden in the center of the floor. There were two cisterns to collect our water supply. Twice a year each was drained, cleaned, and whitewashed to keep the water pure. To ensure we had enough water at all times, only one was cleaned at a time. When it rained, cups placed on gutters on the roof were left turned up until the roof was washed of salt and dirt, then the cups were turned and clean water ran down the gutters and filled the cisterns. We had to be very careful of our water supply, using only that necessary for cooking and keeping clean. In later years I was sailing with friends and short of water when they commented on my rinsing the supper dishes with leftover coffee. My answer: "My lighthouse training."

Our kitchen stove was a Royal Atlantic made of black iron trimmed with nickel. Hot water was held in a two-foot high, eighteen-inch wide, nickelplated copper tank mounted on the back. The stove shone with the stove polish we mixed of boiled oil, turpentine, and lamp black. The nickel was polished with silver polish.

I remembered the deep kitchen windowsills filled with geraniums of all kinds that Minnie had grown, and I followed her example, making the kitchen a bright spot in a barren place. The room was large enough to easily hold an extension table, kitchen chairs, a couch, a comfortable leather chair for Elson by the window, and my cabinet sewing machine. It was truly our living place.

Above the living quarters was the light. Every night we carried a brass can of wood alcohol up the stairs to the light tower. In the room below the lantern we stopped to wind the mechanism which operated the clock that turned the lens. After kerosene was pumped up to a container under the mantel of the lamp, a burning alcohol cup was placed to heat the mantle until it was white hot. Then the kerosene was turned on and the heat vaporized the oil, lighting the light. The lamp took from twenty to thirty minutes to light, so the whole operation had to be timed just right to have the light operating at sundown. It was a matter of great pride to have the light lit at just the moment sunset was declared by the almanac.

We were dedicated enough so that the minute sundown came that light was lit, and the minute the sun rose, it was extinguished. Of course if you were a minute or two ahead of sunset, you could leave the lens cover on or leave the window shades down, but only for a minute or two. Usually the lights were lit right on the dot. All the keepers were as dedicated as we were in this.

The light was a fourth order light. Like Channel Light, it had a Fresnel lens, imported from France and very expensive. Glass prisms pointing down encircled the top of the lens, and more, pointing up, encircled the bottom. They concentrated the light on a convex plain band around the middle of the lens, focusing it into one intense line. The Avery Rock light was a flashing light, so the band in the middle was a series of bull's-eyes which increased the intensity of the light when the lens rotated on its wheels and the beam hit the bull's eyes and flashed. In a fixed or steady light the band in the middle was clear.

I loved being in the tower both to light and to extinguish the lamp. Sometimes the evening was like a series of paintings of perfect sunsets, sometimes nature wrestled with wind, waves, clouds, rain, and snow. At times the surf was too wild to stay and watch.

At sunrise the day came to life, the sun appearing over the islands at the entrance to the bay, then filling the water with diamonds and our home with light. Our job was to extinguish the kerosene lamp and care for the light. Each day the brass the lens was set in was cleaned and polished and the lens covered with its pure linen cover, washed and ironed, without a wrinkle. The windows of the lantern room were washed and the window shades drawn. The lens had to be protected. Finally, the floor and the winding stairs were dusted with a hand brush, the dust caught in a polished, brass dustpan.

After the tower had been taken care of, we ate breakfast, usually hot biscuits or muffins and cereal. I then did the housework and baked what we needed of the bread, doughnuts, biscuits, pies, cakes, and cookies I regularly made. My own work done, I'd often go out to help Elson with the endless painting of the buildings.

A lighthouse keeper had to be a jack-of-all-trades and Elson's tasks were many, so I helped him all I could. At various times he would have to be a painter, carpenter, mechanic, and navigator. Boat engines and boats had to be repaired, ropes on the derrick that lifted the rowboat in the gulch and that hauled our boat up the slip had to be spliced, machinery had to be kept in working order, and the buildings had to be painted yearly to offset the pounding of the weather and sea. I learned to do very few of the tasks, but I did a lot of painting!

We had supper around five o'clock and after washing the dishes, listened to the radio. It was a pleasant surprise if we got KDKA from East Pittsburgh, Pennsylvania, clearly; it was the only station we could receive at Avery. Radio was an infant marvel then. Earphones had to be used, but the wires holding them on the head made ridges, so we could only listen with our twin headsets for a short time before resting.

There was work to be done in the evening also. Elson knit heads for the lobstermen and for the traps he fished. I'd knit socks and the shorter footings to wear inside boots with socks. I made quilts, sheets, and pillow cases. Since we made all our own bedding, I would buy bolts of thirty-six-inch unbleached cotton and sew the widths together with very fine stitching, done over and over. At times we felt we could afford a better white cotton and I'd hemstitch over these sheets and trim them with hand-crocheted lace. I sewed my own everyday dresses on my foot-operated treadle sewing machine. When I tried to make a shirt for Elson, it seemed a work of art until he tried it on and the collar was clearly crooked. He never forgot to tease me about it.

The evening was also the time to write up the log, a daily journal of weather conditions, equipment problems, and incidents or events. Also, the Lighthouse Service required that the log show a ten-day supply of food. Each month a report was sent in to the superintendent's office. A yearly report recorded all use of oil, coal, stationery, paint, and other supplies, and included notes about operation of light buoys and repairs completed or needed.

Getting enough food to eat was a lot of work. We could grow nothing to eat on Avery Rock; there was no soil. With no electricity or refrigeration, we depended for a large part of our diet on food I canned. Aunt Ethel and Elson's grandfather had vegetable gardens and I'd can peas and beans from them. Carrots we would bury in a box of sand we kept in the basement. We had no fresh fruit but a barrel of apples in the cellar. Elson and his grandfather gunned for coots and wild duck and dug pecks of pure, delicious clams on Hog Island, which Grandfather owned. I canned all these, as well as the venison they hunted. Grandfather's weirs gave us food too. When the sardine boats came to seine the weir, Grandfather picked out the large herring and mackerel the sardine men didn't want and sent them out to me to can. My pantry in the cellar really looked appetizing; my pleasure in it paid for the long, hard hours spent preparing it.

Grandfather also raised sheep, so lamb was sent out to us. We kept it fresh for a couple of days by wrapping it in oiled paper, putting it in a leakproof metal container Elson had soldered, and sinking it in the salt water. Fresh chicken and eggs were often sent out by Aunt Ethel. The eggs I intended to use for baking I'd preserve in a brine. Elson's grandmother and aunt were experts at preserving food; meat canned their way tasted almost fresh. I used many of their recipes.

Some food items we bought in bulk and had the cases or hundred-pound bags delivered by the lobster smack which came out from Rockland to buy the lobsters Elson caught. We'd order what we wanted one trip, to be delivered the next time the smack came. Slab bacon, salt pork, sugar, cereal, lard, and dry beans came this way, as did the wooden boxes of canned milk and soda crackers. Other items were not so heavy and Elson bought them at the store in Bucks Harbor.

Sometimes transporting of food and mail was dangerous as well as difficult. One Christmas season Elson had gone into Bucks Harbor for the mail and supplies. When returning to Avery Rock, Elson would ordinarily approach the slip standing, facing the bow as he rowed, so he could jump out as soon as the bow touched the ways and hold the boat as I took a strain on the winch, making taut the line I'd attached to the bow. This time the undertow was vicious and there was very little lull between surges of surf. Just as he put the bow of the boat on the slip, a big wave took the boat off the slip up onto the rocks. Elson ended up half trapped under it. The oars were gone; we never found them. I got the winch rope hooked before another wave could come and move the boat, crushing Elson. But when the next wave came, Elson somehow got the boat clear enough of the rocks so

I could take a strain. He managed to get the boat back on the slip again and, believe me, we worked hard and fast to get it out of danger before the next onslaught of surf!

The boat was two-thirds full of water, and Christmas packages and cans of milk fallen from the case were rolling all over the bottom of the boat. The packages were well wrapped so none were spoiled from the water, but when Elson went to lift the hundred-pound bag of sugar he'd bought, it broke and the liquid sugar ran down all over him. We couldn't even save the syrup, which we might use for pickle brine, though I'd run for cans, hoping to save some of it.

Gram and Granpa used to come out often. Elson was the apple of Granpa's eye and they had a great relationship. One calm winter day, ice covered the rock, building up especially thick on the slip. Granpa wanted some ice cream, so Elson went ashore to get eggs, milk, cream, and the ice cream freezer from his grandparents' house. He also brought ice from the shed where his grandfather packed it in sawdust for his own use. When he came back, I was there to hook the rope to the bow and operate the winch as usual. Everything was going fine when suddenly the boat started sliding back down the iced-up slip like greased lightening. The gears slipped; the handle of the winch turned so fast I couldn't catch it. I reached out to put the clamper down to slow the machine, when somehow my arm got caught.

The force of the contact brought the sliding boat to a halt, but the cogs had done a job on my arm. I was hurt so badly it seemed I could see in back of me as well as in front. I felt like a person watching this happen to me. I have the marks of the cogs on my arm to this day. It was saved from being crushed only by my heavy sweater with the double layer at the cuff.

Gram put iodine on the broken skin and then bandaged it. I walked the floor all night; it wasn't until the next day that Elson could get me ashore to Bucks Harbor. From there I went alone with the mail team the nine miles to the doctor in Machias. Elson had to return to the Rock because Granpa couldn't operate the light and Elson couldn't take the chance of not being able to land later. For six months I couldn't use my arm, but it healed eventually and was normal again.

We couldn't grow food on Avery Rock because of the lack of soil, but something in me wanted some kind of growing thing at our home, some kind of life besides ourselves. So, one day we took all the pails and boxes we could find and my washtubs and went over to Chance's Island. Familiar with the island because we went there for raspberries, I knew we could fill our containers with rich loam. Back on Avery, Elson made a long box along the fence and I planted marigolds, geraniums, and petunias, all of which flourished. I was so proud of my garden!

Then Auntie thought it would be nice if we had a hen and six chicks to raise for food. The only place we had for them to scratch was the ash pile, so Elson built a wire fence around it. One day I went out to pick some flowers, to find them strewn all over the cement patio. In the center of the garden box were the hen and chicks having a wonderful time scratching in the earth. I cried to see the flowers we had worked so hard for, all destroyed. Elson put the hen and chicks in a box and returned them to Auntie to raise for us.

The day Elson handed me a shoe box full of holes and shifting with the weight of something moving inside, I opened it very carefully. He'd been in to Bucks Harbor getting the mail and I didn't know what to expect; Elson loved to play pranks with me. Lifting the lid, I heard the cry of a baby kitten. I held in my hands a ball of fur that needed its mother, so tiny he couldn't walk without falling. When milk was put on the floor for him, he didn't know how to drink. The mother had been killed and the kitten was to have been drowned, until Elson took it. With a medicine dropper, Elson put some of the unfamiliar, warm canned milk in its mouth and we took turns teaching it to drink.

Kitty grew into a fluffy little joy, then into a handsome cat, black with white nose, vest, and four paws he kept gleaming. Elson and I were the only companions he knew. He'd sit beside me when I sat on the rocks and frolic along the rocks when I took a walk. Often he'd get all snarled up in the lines to Elson's traps, or beg for his lobster meat. One day he caught a large, white skate, dragging it up to the house for us to admire. When I was knitting he'd sneak up behind me, reach out a paw and knock the yarn ball off my lap, winding himself up in the wool, causing me to drop stitches before I could retrieve the ball. He had so much fun I couldn't spank him. Soon he'd be nestled in my lap sound asleep.

Avery Rock was often beautiful. On clear, sunny days I loved to take my fancywork or book to the rocks where I could watch the boats going by and look at the scenery. The Rock was about in the center of Machias Bay. To the north were Stone, Salt, and Hog Islands. Beyond Stone Island was the mouth of the Machias River and then Machiasport where Fort O'Brien Park commemorated the first naval battle of the Revolution. I would try to picture the events of this battle, but could not associate them with this calm and peaceful sight. I could not envision the sloop *Unity* capturing the larger *Margaretta* on June 12, 1775. Even though Elson's family owned the powder horn that had belonged to Timothy Libby, the boy the English sailors forced to tell them where Fort O'Brien was located, I could not make the events real to me as I looked out over the bay.

To the east of the Rock was Holmes Bay and Cutler, a thickly wooded point used as a pasture, and good blueberry land. Half a mile away was Chance's Island where we would beach the powerboat when she needed a new shaft or a paint job, and where we got our raspberries for jam and sauce. Out of Avery was the Coast Guard station on Cross Island, then the Libby Island Light. To the west was the town of Starboard, and Bar and Bear Islands and Yellow Head, all owned by Elson's family.

The river appeared so calm, but the undertow would surge around our slip and in the gulch where we landed when we couldn't get on the slip. We often scanned the water to see if any boats needed help. One nice day there was a fresh north wind blowing as I looked out over the bay. About a mile above the Rock an empty rowboat bobbed up and down. I knew this belonged to Mr. Pettigrew and feared he'd fallen overboard when he pulled his traps. When Elson returned from shore with the mail, he went up to check the boat which was anchored, all in order. Just then a powerboat with Mr. Pettigrew aboard came alongside. It seemed he'd been taken ill and hailed a powerboat to take him ashore, where he'd felt better and had now returned for his boat. It was an unusual occurrence and gave Elson and me a turn.

Another day I checked the bay and saw a beautiful buck deer standing at the foot of the steps. After resting a while he gracefully leapt into the water. I watched him swim to the mainland.

The calm days were rare. We could never leave the

Rock unattended for more than a few hours for fear that a sudden bad spell would prevent one of us from being there to light the lamp at sunset. The Rock was treacherous to land at in poor weather, sometimes getting on the slip was impossible and we'd have to go into the gulch.

We hadn't been at Avery Rock long when Elson decided he needed better and quicker transportation for going after mail and supplies than the rowboat with its sail, a good seaworthy craft, but heavy for one man to handle. So, in March of 1923, he bought a Jonesport powerboat for $250, a lot of money to us. One Saturday he took it to Machias to have it fitted for a spray hood and cover, while I stayed at home to tend the light as a storm was brewing.

The waves were pretty high when I saw him, a white speck coming between the islands above the light. By the time he made the mooring, the waves were very high and I was uneasy. Usually I loved to watch him bring the boat to just the right position to catch the mooring line, but I feared that today he'd have a bad time making the slip. The surf broke across the slip and all over us as I stood ready to hook the line on the bow of the rowboat Elson had brought in from the mooring.

Elson stood facing the bow while I ran back up the slip to take the strain on the winch. As I turned the winch he hollered to me, "Connie, put the clamp down on the winch and go up to the house and shut the shutters. We're in for a tough nor'easter."

I yelled back that I'd already closed the shutters and had also turned the cups to the cisterns. Elson winched the boat up into the boathouse, fearing it wasn't safe to leave it out, and then proceeded to batten down any movable thing outside.

At one end of the house, by the bell tower, a huge bulkhead constructed in a V shape pointed out to the water to cut the force of the sea. Made of eight-by-eight hard pine spiked together and spiked into the rock with iron bolts, it was ten to fifteen feet high, each side of the V about twenty feet long. The sea struck the bulkhead sending spray over the house and the tower. In storms we closed the shutters on all the windows but one, that the kitchen window and farthest from the breaking sea. Through this window we would watch the storm, though even the glass was covered by blowing surf much of the time.

That Saturday there was a period of almost three hours when the raging water at our door prevented us from getting out of the house. We had to wait until the tide ebbed, reducing the sea. I went up to the tower, but it was too bad to stay. The sea flung itself at the windows; I felt the vibrations of its force. I was really frightened. This was a line gale and a bad one.

All day Sunday we felt the power of the sea. From our one unshuttered window we watched the spray fill our boat as she rose and fell on the waves. We could see the water rush from bow to stern over the engine and Elson knew he was going to lose his boat. It would be a transportation loss as well as a financial one.

About 8:45 A.M. on Monday, a big surge of spray hit and we saw her sink. Elson turned away, very sorrowful. When the spray cleared from our window, I could see she was floating, though straight up and down. Excitedly I said, "Come here, Elson. The boat didn't sink — I can see about two feet of her bow out of the water."

Elson happily hurried back, but when he watched her rising and falling in the deep trough, he said, "I'm afraid if this keeps up much longer her stern will be battered to pieces."

Not long after, we saw the Coast Guard lifeboat from the Cross Island Station coming toward the light. A welcome sight, the crew had come to see if we survived the storm. Elson's father turned out to be on the boat, though we hadn't been able to get our mail for several days and didn't know at the time that he'd been transferred from New Hampshire to Cross Island. The crew couldn't get near the Rock, but by megaphone told Elson they'd rescue his boat, and proceeded to tow it bottom up to Bucks Harbor.

Three days later Elson could finally launch the rowboat to get to Bucks Harbor where he found that the engine had been dried out and was ready for him. His father and grandfather had even saved most of the gas by straining the water out using chamois.

When there was a big storm like this one, some major damage was usually done. This time the boat slip and part of the boat house washed away. Although Elson could do the minor repairs, this type of job necessitated a crew of men: three carpenters, a boss carpenter, and an engineer. We were supposed to furnish beds and board them. The only money we received was $1.18 a day for each one's meals. Since we also furnished our own dwellings, this meant they used our furniture and bedding and other belongings, for which no allowance was given. Nor was there any compensation for my doing the laundry for three beds and the towels for five men, all of which was done by hand with a scrub board and tub and a boiler on the stove to boil the clothes to keep them white and sanitary.

With no electricity, refrigeration, or outside communication, I wondered how I was going to feed seven people on this desolate rock. Each meal was hearty. Bacon, eggs, hash brown potatoes, hot biscuits freshly baked every morning, doughnuts, and coffee with canned milk made up breakfast. One of the carpenters loved doughnuts. He'd take one and break it into three pieces and fit them between his knuckles while he took another to eat. I wondered why he did this for he was welcome, at least in our house, to have as many as he wanted.

For dinner and the evening meal my canned things came into good use. If we couldn't get fresh meat or fish, we used canned, as well as canned vegetables and the stored carrots, potatoes, or turnips. The noon dinner always ended with pie and we always had cake and cookies at the evening meal. No one bought store bread or other baked things in those days; you were considered lazy if you bought a loaf of bread.

Saturday nights I heated gallons of water so all the men could take their baths. They built an enclosure around the furnace in the basement where they used my washtub to bathe in. Through the week they had a pitcher of water and a bowl in their rooms to do their daily washing.

One of the carpenters in the crew was Cliff Turner, who was to start his furlough to be married while at Avery. For two days before he was to leave, it stormed, and a heavy sea covered the Rock. Anxiously he watched, hoping it would be calm enough for Elson to get him ashore. The morning he was to leave he was certain he was not going to attend his own wedding, but Elson told him that if he was brave enough and felt he wanted to take the chance, "I will get you ashore."

Since the slip had been washed away and not yet rebuilt, Elson had brought the rowboat around in the gulch and hoisted it up on the davit above the surf.

Elson and Howard Colbath, the boss carpenter, lowered the boat, then Elson and Cliff jumped aboard, Howard and another man waiting for the signal to cast off the ropes. Cliff held onto the thwart in the stern, Elson held the oars poised, ready to row the boat through the breaking surf at just the right minute. Suddenly, he started rowing. I could not watch. That boat was literally standing on end and I feared they would be dashed on the rocks and drowned. Mr. Lunt, one of the carpenters, was a kind man and came to sit beside me, trying to calm me. The engineer of the group watched at the window. Finally, he turned and told me, "You can breathe now, Connie. They're through the surf and rowing toward shore." After that experience I never doubted Elson could handle even a situation beyond human strength and sea power.

Naturally, our lives were controlled by the weather and we never knew what it would be. One late fall day I stood on the rocks looking at the islands that seemed so near in the clear atmosphere created by the fresh north winds. The sea was so calm that the islands were difficult to distinguish from their reflections on the water. Land and water seemed joined. I thought of a big fish, split down its stomach and laid flat so the two sides made one large, many-colored, iridescent mat.

Elson came out of the workshop where he'd been repairing some machinery and stood beside me. When I told him my feeling about the reflections, he said, "You know, Connie, when you see weather like this it means we're going to have a storm. The wind will change and we'll get some soft weather."

Even as we watched, feathery streaks of clouds were beginning to creep in over the sky, the clear air becoming hazy. The next day, sure enough, the wind was from the south. The atmosphere was a green haze and the waves got higher and higher. I went out on the rocks by the house and looked down the bay. No land was visible. The green sea washed across the rocks, the tops of the huge waves whipped by the wind.

I couldn't believe my eyes when a three-masted vessel, all sails flying, came like a streak out of the haze, bobbing up and down on the waves. I hollered to Elson to come see if I was seeing right. The vessel was not in the channel and was headed to a sandbar about a half-mile above us. Elson was very concerned; he made about a hundred trips from the house to the boat house wishing he could somehow warn the ship, wondering why she was on that side of the Rock. But he couldn't launch a boat in this weather, so we could only hope the ship would be all right.

The vessel anchored, and the sails were lowered, so we decided the captain had found solid ground bottom, though Elson said it was too sandy a place for a ship to anchor and was afraid the anchor would drag. Soon we saw the vessel was dragging her anchor and coming straight for Avery Rock. Again Elson paced the rocks, but just before the ship reached us, we saw the Coast Guard boat coming. The crew had come to investigate why the vessel was in the area and towed her to a safe place, where she anchored for several days.

As soon as Elson could launch a boat he went aboard the vessel, finding to his amazement, that the captain was the one he had sailed with on a couple of trips to Rotterdam. He had been an excellent captain, whom Elson had liked, but had developed a drinking problem. He'd had to leave the other vessel and had taken this one in New York. So the mystery as to why the vessel almost wrecked on Avery Rock was solved.

I was left on the Rock most of the times Elson went ashore so I could operate the light in case he couldn't make it back. Though I could run the light and the bell, Elson never taught me how to fix the machinery, since he always did that. One winter, two weeks of bad weather meant no mail and a low stock of supplies. The wind was southeast with a fresh breeze and the sky was lowering. Even though there was quite a swell, Elson decided he'd have to go ashore, rowing the heavy tender, or rowboat, he used in winter, the three miles to Bucks Harbor. I really felt uneasy.

He'd been gone about an hour when it began to snow and shut in thick. I wound the winch-like handle that started the bell that was used in fog and snow, and proceeded to keep busy so I wouldn't worry. Suddenly, I realized the bell wasn't going. It was funny, but we seemed to have an inner warning system. We'd be asleep on a foggy night when the bell signal was in operation and Elson would suddenly jump out of bed. I'd know at once that the bell had stopped. Now, when I realized its absence, I went quickly up into the bell tower attached to the side of the house. To my dismay, the machine had broken down. What was I to do? Fishermen, Coast Guard crews, and, of course, Elson were somewhere out there in the snow, needing the bell to sound in the pattern or characteristic which would tell them which lighthouse they were approaching. I untied the ropes we used to ring the bell by hand when we saluted the lighthouse tender and began to pull, counting: one — zero — two — zero — three — zero — and so on until I thought fifteen seconds had gone by, then another pull to get the two strokes every fifteen seconds which was the characteristic of Avery Rock.

I pulled the ropes steady for one and a half hours until

my hands were so blistered I couldn't pull another stroke. I stopped. I looked all over the floor of the tower; under the machine I saw a cotter pin. Elson kept the place so spotless and tidy that it was easy to determine the pin hadn't just been dropped there; I knew it must be out of the machine somewhere. I was praying hard that no one was near the rock without the bell, for now there was quite a surf. It was almost thirty minutes since the bell had stopped. I started looking for holes that the cotter pin would fit, but nowhere would that pesky pin go in. On my knees, looking up under the machine, I saw that the hammer arm had dropped down out of place and when I finally got it in line, the pin went right in. I wound the mechanism that operated the bell, and, lo, it went perfect. What a relief!

Elson came home about half an hour later. I ran to the boat house so I could be on the slip to hook the line to the bow of the rowboat. We worked fast to get the boat safe, for the sea was rushing across the slip and we had to secure her between surges of surf.

Elson had been just coming around the island when he missed the bell. When I asked how he ever found the Rock, he said, "I knew the wind direction, the direction the rock was, and as I rowed I'd stop, wet my finger, hold it up, and when I felt the wind, I'd know."

I'd never heard of this method before and thought he was kidding me. He told me, "I was some glad to hear the bell. I was afraid something had happened to you."

Fortunately there were very few times when something did happen to us or when we were sick. Elson always protected me as much as possible from the serious things in life, and since we were almost always together, I seldom had to deal with dangerous situations myself. When something did happen I had to use my own ingenuity to solve a problem; I didn't have time to look up the answer; I didn't have time to get instructions. I had to do it because things happened so quickly I had to do the best I could. I might not have been qualified to do something and yet I had to do it. So I got used to it: I just stepped over the line and did what had to be done.

One memorable time, Elson had a bad cold which developed into a fever of 103 degrees. I couldn't summon a doctor for the only way was to ring the bell — if it would even be heard three miles away on the mainland — and at this time it was officially in use for a snowstorm raging outside. The sea was too rough for me to launch the boat, so I studied the medical book to find something I could give him to break the fever. The book said quinine. I gave him the dose recommended and he became so delirious I couldn't keep him in bed, so I wrapped him in a blanket and sat him with his feet up on the oven hearth. He soaked all the clothes I could get on him and shook so hard I was frightened. I finally got him to bed and quieted, but it was four days before he gained enough strength to make me feel he was on the mend. Fortunately, he liked gruel made of cornmeal cooked a long time, then thinned with milk, so I fed him that. It wasn't until the medicine chest was renewed later that I learned a mistake had been made in the power of the quinine; the pills were double the regular dose.

I surely thanked the Lord for Elson's recovery. I had thought he was going to die. It was twelve days before he was well enough to tend the light and during this time I was responsible for running it. Snow fell heavily for two days, then a bad spell of weather lasted a week. I kept asking myself, "Can I do it? Can I do it?" I managed to keep the bell and light operating, but by the time Elson was able to go into the tower I had come down with the same sickness. I tried not to give in to it and worry Elson, but as I sat playing caroms with him, his face was just a blur. I took his temperature and became panicky; when I put the thermometer in his mouth I knew it had registered below ninety-eight degrees but when I took it out I couldn't even see the mercury. I told myself to calm down, it surely hadn't gone so high it was out of sight. I took a breath and looked again to find that it registered 103 degrees. You just have to talk to yourself in cases like that in order to operate efficiently.

The worst storm happened after we left Avery Rock. In January 1927, Captain Sherman of the Lighthouse Service stopped at Seguin Light, where Elson was head keeper, to tell us of the damage done to Avery Rock during a heavy gale and terrific surf. The huge bulkhead was torn up by the surf, part of it wrecking the bell house, then crashing through the thick wooden shutters into the bedroom, opening a clear path for the sea to flood the house. The keeper, Mr. Edward Pettigrew, bored holes in the floor, letting the water go into the basement, which of course flooded the furnace. Mr. Pettigrew, his wife, and aged mother had to huddle in a corner of the kitchen by the stove for the three days the storm lasted, all the time scared to death. As Mr. Pettigrew said later, "If it had lasted another hour and a half we would have been lost. " Captain Sherman told us their bed was unrecognizable, a mass of twisted iron. We missed this storm by only six months. I have stood on the steps of the house at Avery and watched the green sea flow across the rocks directly in front and this was bad enough for me.

After being on Avery Rock for a while, I began to feel

very lonely. I needed to see and talk to someone. Anyone! At first I was so busy getting our home organized and learning the ways of lighthouse living, I was content to let this fill my days. And, I was simply happy that Elson and I were together. But I began to feel I needed something besides my housework, and the knitting, crocheting, and other handwork I did. Browsing through the little library provided by the Lighthouse Service and changed periodically when the tenders arrived, I came across two small booklets called "The Message" and "Deeds of Valor of the Coast Guard and Lighthouse Men." They both interested me very much, so I decided to write to Mr. Edward Law, the author of "The Message." To my surprise, he answered my letter and a very fine friendship grew between Mr. Law and Elson and me.

An ordained minister living in Detroit, Michigan, Mr. Law, with his wife, also conducted a mission for Indians and needy people. He extended this mission to Coast Guard and Lighthouse Service people after he and his sons were rescued by the Coast Guard when they were sailing his yacht *Dream* on one of the Great Lakes on their mission work and were wrecked. He almost drowned and was resuscitated by a Coast Guard crew; he said it was easy going out, but when they brought him back it was painful. He was so grateful to the Coast Guard that each year he would prepare a message to send to all the Coast Guard and lighthouse people. He helped many of them who were unfortunate financially since there was no aid or pensions for them from the government. Mr. Law also worked with Congress to better the pay and improve living conditions.

When Mr. Law suggested that I write to those on the list of missions and isolated lighthouses he sent me, the old urge to write came back. Besides the writing I did as a young person, I had written a story and sent it to the Palmer Photoplay Studio in Hollywood when we were first married. I took a test as to my ability to write scenarios and passed, and was recommended to enter school for instruction to write scripts. But the school was far away and costly; besides, I had a husband to take care of who didn't want his wife to have any career but for him. So, I gave up all idea of writing.

But this correspondence with missions and lighthouses would not cause me to neglect Elson; while he listened to the radio and knit the heads and pockets for the lobster fishermen in the evenings, I racked my brains for something interesting to write about.

Now when Elson brought home the crocus sacks, the burlap sugar sacks he used to carry mail in, there was usually more than the newspapers and magazines we subscribed to or which were sent free to lighthouses. Now I looked forward to more than the latest adventures of Stella Dallas in serial form in the Boston American newspaper, which we eagerly awaited. When Elson brought home the first mail we'd had in ten or fifteen days, he'd dump the sacks, as many as four, in the middle of the kitchen floor, and we'd start sorting, beginning our reading of letters with the oldest. I'd have as many as twenty-five letters from missions and lights all over the world. The people I corresponded with were just as isolated as we were, or more so. I remember especially the letters from Tillamook Light off the coast of Oregon and those from a light in Alaska where the keepers got mail but once a year. The people I corresponded with in England, Italy, Africa, India, the North American coasts, Canada, the Caribbean, and other places would find interesting subjects to write to me in their isolation and I was always challenged in answering them. I had many happy hours visiting with my penpals. I kept only two letters, one from Mr. Law and one from a Mr. Strain, who was head of the lighthouse mission in Northern Ireland.

Mr. Law visited us on Avery Rock and again later on Seguin. He had never seen the rise and fall of the tide or a lobster fresh from the sea. You would see him and Kitty sitting side by side for long periods, fascinated by the sea. When Elson threw lobsters from the boat onto the rocks before he plugged them, Mr. Law started to pick one up by the claw. I yelled at him not to touch it, scaring the poor man half to death before I could explain that had he picked it up he would have been pinched very badly.

The Machias Seal Islands were twelve miles straight out to sea from us; the light was a Canadian one on an island owned by the United States. Mr. Law was anxious to see the islands because he had helped the families on them. Elson said he would take him, so they left early one morning in our little twenty-six-foot Jonesport boat, coincidentally named *Dream*, as was Mr. Law's sailboat. There was a heavy breeze that day, and I paced the rocks most of the time while they were gone, until I finally saw them come through Cross Island Narrows, making a white path as they hit the waves. They were able to land all right, though Mr. Law said, "My beloved Elson is a great boatman, but I never thought I'd be so happy to be safe on a bunch of rocks as I am right now." The visit had been very rewarding to Mr. Law, but the trip back was very rough.

Despite my letters to and from the missions and light-houses, I still sometimes got lonely. Usually it was Elson who went ashore because he could handle the boat easily. The little I did go ashore, we went to Aunt Ethel's or other family members' homes, or to the post office or to visit a woman friend of mine in Bucks Harbor. We also went to other islands to pick berries. One rare calm Sunday, I was alone on the Rock and went outside to enjoy the weather. Elson had gone ashore to pick some vegetables at his grandfather's. I sat on the railing looking across to Larrabee, the only place there was an opening to the road where cars whizzed by. I wondered what was so important to the people in them that they rushed so. I could see the home of Elson's uncle, Clair Berry, where we had happy times when we rowed over. I had a warm spot in my heart for his young son, Kenneth, who was always pleased when we rowed to visit and who made us feel we were very special because we lived in a lighthouse.

I walked down to the rocks, all dressed up in my Sunday clothes, a pretty georgette blouse embroidered with blue flowers, a blue straw hat with peacock feathers, a skirt of deeper blue. A phrase ran through my mind, "all dressed up and no place to go."

I picked up a periwinkle and watched him crawl back into his shell, afraid of strange surroundings. I thought, "I don't have to be lonely with a world of different creatures to be explored." Somehow, I felt less alone, but it would have been very nice if I could have heard other human voices. Then I saw Elson coming around the islands in *Dream*. I wasn't lonely anymore; he would be bringing me fresh news from family and friends.

Sometimes we had surprise visitors. One morning we had gotten up to extinguish the light at sunrise when Elson called down to me that the lighthouse tender was heading for the Rock and to get things done up before they reached us. As they landed, we saw that not one, but two inspectors were coming ashore. Mr. Sampson had been appointed as Assistant Superintendent of the First Lighthouse District, and Mr. Luther, the Superintendent of Engineering and former Assistant, was escorting him around to the lights. And so, at six o'clock in the morning, I was having an inspection of our living quarters.

Each year a star was issued to those lights that passed inspection. A commissioner's star went to those who passed inspection for three years, and the station considered to have improved most and which had already been given the commissioner's star was given the district pennant, the highest award issued.

One day Elson returned from shore very pleased, for he had been awarded the pennant. It was to be flown whenever a tender was spotted coming to the light, but at Avery Rock there was no pole or place outside where we could fly it, so we fixed a wall in the tower room and displayed it there. Mr. Sampson came on inspection and was some annoyed when he landed, for he didn't see the pennant flying for him. But his mood improved when he saw what Elson had done and why, and he was pleased. Elson was awarded the pennant for three years before we moved to Seguin.

There were definite steps to advancement in the Lighthouse Service. First or second assistant keepers were assigned to remote and isolated stations. After proving they could successfully survive this probation period, they could select the station they would accept a transfer to. I can remember us spreading charts on the kitchen floor and discussing the pros and cons of this station or that one.

As it turned out, we spent time on only two of the stations we listed. Elson did not want to go to a two or three-man station, but after four years on Avery Rock, Captain Sherman, the Superintendent of the First Lighthouse District, asked Elson if he would accept a transfer to Seguin Light at the mouth of the Kennebec River. Elson did not want to go to this three-man light, but Captain Sherman felt that as head keeper Elson could correct some problems at the light. Elson felt he should accept, and did.

We received notice that the tender would arrive at Avery Rock on July 15, 1926, to pick up our furniture and move us to Seguin. We started moving the furniture to the boat house where Elson made a sort of a platform to set it on in case there was a storm and water came into the building. With six rooms in the house, we had accumulated quite a lot of furniture.

It had been perfect weather, so Elson suggested we clean and polish everything in the house and move into the boat house for the couple of days left until the tender arrived. Since the boat house floor was on a slant, he leveled the oil stove, table, and bed. To make it more like a camping holiday, we built a small fire between the rocks and cooked our food there, lighting the oil stove only to heat our bath water and make our tea and coffee. It was a wonderful experience to sleep at night with the tide and surf splashing up under the floor. Many nights at the house on Avery Rock I'd fallen asleep to the music of the lapping of the water flowing in and out over the rocks outside our bedroom window. Avery Rock was the only light we lived at where the living quarters were near enough to the water to hear this sound. I missed it a lot when I left there and can still hear it in memory.

The fifteenth arrived and passed, with no tender. We began to get uneasy, our sense of peace and relaxation invaded by questions about what had happened and whether we would be lucky enough to continue to have the beautiful weather. Elson decided to go ashore for mail and supplies, for our provisions were getting low. When he returned and read the mail, we learned there had been a change and the tender would not arrive until the twenty-third, eight days away.

Elson dealt with every situation in a very practical way, so he said, "We have everything in order to leave, there are no predicted storms, so we'll just relax and enjoy every minute we can. If it storms, we'll take two sections off the bed-couch and spread it on the floor in the kitchen of the house to sit and sleep on. We have our papers, books, and checker game. We'll row over to Chance's Island to pick raspberries if they're ripe and the surf calm. I have material to knit heads and you can do your crocheting while we listen to the radio, and I'll play the banjo to you." He made it sound like paradise.

It really was a delightful ten days. The night of the twenty-third, we saw the tender off Libby Island. At about eleven o'clock the next morning it arrived at the Rock with the relief keeper on board. Our utopia was over.

I was excited to be aboard a large ship and at the prospect of seeing more of the coast of Maine I had read so much about. I planned to write to all my penpals, describing all the lighthouses we would pass.

Steaming down Machias Bay, watching Avery Rock grow smaller and smaller, I reviewed the four years I had lived there. Elson came and stood at the rail beside me. I knew what he was thinking. "Well, Connie, our first home is fading into the blue of the bay and the sky. These four years were priceless because we found happiness and companionship in simple living, and strength to combat adversity. I almost feel I'm abandoning the light we tended so carefully and took so much pride in. We'll be going into a different way of living, associating with many types of people. I hope we never lose the closeness to each other and the beauty we had on Avery Rock." But he was a man of few words. After a while he said, "You made it a great time."

I looked at him, squeezed his hand, and said, "Thank you, Elson, for saying that. But, we must remember that it takes two to achieve this. If times get hard and complicated, we know we have each other to talk things over with, to resolve problems with."

We waved to all our dear ones in Larrabee, Bucks Harbor, and Starboard, even though we knew they couldn't see us this far from land. Then we turned to wave to the lightkeepers and their families on Libby Island as we passed it. I looked out across the ocean and barely able to pick out Machias Seal Island thought what a long trip it had been for Elson and Mr. Law. Now the ocean showed whitecaps as the rays of the late afternoon sun reflected iridescent colors dancing to and fro.

Captain Faulkingham headed for Jonesport where we anchored for the night. Born in Jonesport, he was a favorite son and it was exciting to see the people lining the shore, waving as he blew the whistle in answer to their greetings. The next morning at sunrise we were on our way again. Even at five o'clock in the morning people were there to wave good-bye.

I was glad Captain Faulkingham was taking the coastal route. I could already see the next lighthouse appear on the horizon; Moose Peak, situated on Mistake Island. In nearer shore, at the entrance to Harrington Bay, was Nash Island Light. Way out in the ocean I saw what looked like a tall mast sticking up out of the water, but when we drew nearer it turned out to be Petit Manan Light. The island was so low and flat that I wondered what the keepers and their families experienced when the sea was rough. As this was the second highest light on the Maine coast at 123 feet, I thought of the keepers climbing all those stairs to the top every night carrying a five-gallon can of kerosene.

Prospect Harbor Light was next. Then, when we'd sailed around the point, I could see Winter Harbor Light on Mark Island, just off the town of Winter Harbor. From there we passed Schoodic Point, part of Acadia Park and site of a National Park Service station. I could now look up Frenchman's Bay to Bar Harbor, headquarters of the Sea Coast Mission. Egg Rock Light, almost as isolated as Avery, stood at the entrance to the bay.

The Maine coast is like a tattered piece of cloth with points of land and bays constantly jutting in and out of the coastline, necessitating all these lights, as well as many buoys. There were so many lights, I couldn't remember names and locations, so I borrowed a chart from Captain Faulkingham and logged every one I could see.

We were headed for the Bear Island supply depot since the tender crew was taking aboard supplies to be delivered and buoys to replace damaged ones that would be taken to the Portland headquarters for repair. On our way to Bear we passed the lovely summer homes of the Rockefellers, Fords, Welches, and other families, nestled in the woods overlooking the ocean. Out to sea was Baker Island Light just off Islesboro and Cranberry Isle, where the Coast Guard had a station.

We tied up at Bear Island quite a while as supplies were loaded, and cleaned and painted buoys fastened in place on deck. I felt like a queen in my deck chair in the stern looking at the scenery. It was so lovely I didn't want to leave to go to the dining room for lunch. We paid for our meals on board and were served by the steward. I remember still the large bowl of fresh fruit on the buffet, the melon so delicately pink and tasty. Fresh fruit was a real treat.

At last we were under way again. I ran for my chart, pad, and pencil. Bass Harbor Head Light, near McKinley and one of the most photographed lights on the coast, was next. Several miles out to sea was Great Duck Island Light where birds had flown into the tower, breaking all the windows. Far out to sea, twenty miles out, was Mount Desert Light; I thought that the keepers could probably tell some hair-raising tales of the storms there.

I was astonished at the number of little islands and buoys we passed; they reminded me of Cheerios floating in a pan of milk. There were as many buoys as islands in the narrow passage near Stonington on Deer Isle, famous for its granite business, as shown by the derricks and blocks of granite we could see. Below Deer Isle was Mark Island Light just as we came out of the reach into Penobscot Bay. I looked up the bay to Eagle Island Light where my sister Minnie was now living with her family.

Way up the bay were Dices Head Light at Castine, Fort Point Light at the mouth of the Penobscot, and Grindle Point Light on Islesboro. Heading for Rockland for the night, we passed Vinalhaven and then the Rockland Breakwater Light, built on a stone breakwater that reached nearly a mile from shore. Tired that night, we did not go ashore, but stayed in our nice quarters, resting for the next busy day.

We were up early and on deck for a beautiful sunrise, the captain and crew already prepared for the trip to

Seguin. Passing Owls Head Light, nestled in the spruce on the high bluff, we waved to the keeper and his family at Brown's Head Light. Way out to sea was Matinicus Light.

The tender was heading for Two Bush Light, where the captain was to establish a buoy on an uncharted ledge just discovered. The mate called "hitch-main" or "hitch-a-fore" as the crew directed the crane holding the huge piece of granite fastened to the spar buoy with heavy chains. The crane swung the buoy, which weighed tons, over the side, and the mate gave the order to drop it in the exact spot it was to be placed. Everything looked fine and the tall spar stood erect when suddenly there was a loud noise and the buoy disappeared. The weight had caught on the shelf of the ledge, then slid off into deep water. The crew had to reset it; it stayed in place.

As we passed the lights at Marshall Point, Port Clyde, Pemaquid Point, Whitehead, Franklin Island, Ram Island, Monhegan, Burnt Island, and the Cuckolds, the keepers, and especially their children, waved and rang their bells, Captain Faulkingham saluting back with the tender's whistle. This was similar to the Lighthouse Service's regulations requiring keepers to respond to a tender's salute. If there was no salute from the light, the question was, "Where is the keeper? He should be there." Even a stag or one-man light was not supposed to be left alone, but the keeper had to go for supplies occasionally. On a family light, a member of the family was expected to take over; no extra money was paid for this service.

After the Cuckolds was Seguin Light, opposite Popham Beach. Standing on the deck, I finally looked at the place we were to spend the next four years.

S E G U I N

We anchored in a good-sized cove with ledges to the east of us and a bluff to the west. High over us on the bluff was the light, 180 feet above sea level. Seguin was a large island which, when seen from the air, resembled a beaver or Davy Crockett's coonskin cap.

Amidst a lot of activity on deck, our furniture was loaded aboard the supply boat. I made sure Kitty was brought on deck in his box so he would know we were near him. Captain Faulkingham came to say good-bye, making us feel real special when he said he was glad to have had us aboard and wished us a happy stay in our new assignment. Then he added, "Don't look for me to visit you. I'm afraid of snakes." I wondered about the snakes, but soon enough learned that the island was infested with them and that one could fill a large can with them in a short time, something I decided I wouldn't want to try. Captain Faulkingham never did come up to the house, but always sent his greetings by the mate.

We landed on the slip and walked by the donkey house

to a railway built on tresses which were twenty feet high in some places. Called the tramway, it went to the top of the island where the lighthouse, dwellings, and fog signal were situated. The donkey house did not house donkeys, but a powerful engine which operated the cars that hauled the freight, coal, and supplies to the top. Our furniture went up this way.

We walked up the tramway, releasing Kitty as soon as we reached the top. He stood bewildered — he had never seen grass or felt the earth beneath his paws. After a few seconds he scampered away, sliding back and forth through the grass, then returning to our feet, exhausted but very happy in his new world.

The view from the high ground was magnificent. I could see for miles, from Portland Head to Pemaquid Point. Elson walked with me to the house so we could enter together, then he left to help with the landing of our possessions and to survey what he was to assume charge of that day.

The house was a duplex brick building with three ells attached. We entered a shed-like room, used as a utility room, and went into the ell which was the kitchen. On the first floor were the dining room, living room, and a long hall. The second floor had two large bedrooms and at the head of the stairs, an alcove I used as a den. The only light in the halls was from a skylight in the roof. Later, a bay window was built across the bedroom and hall, giving us much-needed light and air, as well as improving the looks of the house outside.

The kitchen had just a black iron stove, a sink with a hand pump, and a small closet. We could put a rocking chair in the space in front of the stove. Elson's grandmother and grandfather had given us a kitchen cabinet for our wedding gift. It had a place for everyday dishes, a drawer for silver and another for utensils, and two drawers for towels. A door on the left opened to a built-in flour sifter and bin. We ate breakfast on the enamel shelf that pulled out. Below the shelf was a breadboard for rolling out biscuits, doughnuts, or cookies. It was an ideal, compact piece of furniture for this small kitchen.

We would have to buy a linoleum carpet for the floor — the one we had on Avery Rock was much too large — that we could put in the dining room to wire my braided scatter rugs. The rest of the rooms were bare, waiting for us to provide our own furnishings. As I walked through the rooms, I furnished them in my mind.

A door in the front hall led into a second hall where supplies for operating the light were kept. A door from this hall opened to the winding iron stairs to the landing, where the mechanism for the light stood, and then into the lantern room itself.

I opened the outside tower entrance door which looked over the north part of the island to Popham Beach and the entrance to the Kennebec River. To the right of the door was the third ell containing the kitchen to the first assistant's living quarters. Our quarters were pleasant, with views of the ocean, islands, and the mainland.

I had no more finished my inspection of the house when our furniture was carried in. In the rush to get everything in place and under cover before night, I completely forgot about lunch until Elson came in hungry. The food I had kept handy for use until we'd settled in was quickly unpacked; then I went to the storage shed for fuel for the coal cookstove. There was no sign of fuel. The previous keeper had used all the coal allowance issued to him and now there would be no more delivered until the last of August, over a month away. It was a funny feeling not to have anything to build a fire with, to heat or cook with.

Elson came to my rescue by breaking up wooden boxes he emptied of books to get enough wood to cook our lunch, but immediately after we finished eating, I decided to drop everything and search for driftwood. Kitty and I made a trip around the shore; he wanted to stay close in this strange place, but loved exploring the rocks.

I didn't find any driftwood and went back to the little beach by the boat house. The tender and crew had gone, so I walked over the beach examining the shells and rocks as I always loved to do. I picked up a stone about the size of an egg, very smooth and light in weight, black with a gray tinge. It fascinated me, so I gathered my apron full and went up the hill to ask Elson what they were. He identified the stones as coal that had been washed for years by the sea, left from the many coal vessels wrecked on Seguin. When we tried burning the coal, we were overjoyed by the warmth from the fire. After that, I would make a daily trip at a certain time of tide to collect what had washed up on the beach that day. What I didn't collect would wash back into the cove with the tide. The Lord certainly provided us with our daily bread!

The second assistant keeper lived in the dwelling next to the whistle, or foghorn. Run by compressed air, the whistle was so powerful that when it blew, the window-panes in our house, some two hundred or more feet away, could be felt to move. People in the second assistant's house would have to stop conversations when it went off. Actually the house, a single-family dwelling, had been meant for the head keeper, but being less than desirable because of the horn, it was used by the keeper last in seniority, the second assistant.

The light at Seguin was one of the most powerful lights on the coast. Twelve feet high and six feet in diameter, the Fresnel lens was large enough for the men to go inside it to light the lamp. Like the whole station, the tower was immaculate. The lens cover of linen, twelve feet long with four sections about six feet wide, had a drawstring at the top which fit over the top of the lens. The cover came down over the lens and fastened at the bottom with another drawstring. It was necessary to use a ladder to reach the top to fasten and drop the cover. I washed and ironed that cover by hand with a tub and tub board and irons that heated on the stove. I was lucky to have a set of irons with a nickel cover that went over each iron and snapped into holes on the sides with two pins. They were quite an improvement over the old flatirons whose handles were so hot a holder had to be used to protect my hands. Still, it was a struggle to iron this linen fabric, so long and wide and difficult to get free of wrinkles, which scorched and yellowed so easily. Elson wanted the lens cover just so, but then, having everything in perfect shape was one of the main duties of keeping a light.

I loved being in the tower at sunset. When I took that lens cover off and the light flashed, I could begin counting from Portland to Pemaquid Point as almost simultaneously the lights came on — thirteen of them. It was like saying, "hello," "hello," "hello," "hello," all down the coast. I felt that spiritually we visited with the people in all of those lights, we knew they were trying to do the same thing we were, protecting navigation. For what was the whole sum and substance of our job, to keep the light going when it should, for there was someone out there who would be running for the light. If it wasn't in proper operating order or wasn't lit, there was trouble. The lights were lifelines to the sailors and navigators.

The first night on Seguin, I went out to see how the light looked. The fog had closed in all around me, making me feel like I was under a huge umbrella, for the rays from the light looked like rivers and streams radiating out. At first I thought stars were moving about, but I soon learned the stars were birds of all kinds attracted to the light. I became accustomed to going out in the mornings and finding twenty-five to forty birds, killed when they flew into the tower: thistle birds or gold-finches, Baltimore orioles, red-winged blackbirds, and others of more common colors. I'd carefully put them in a box and bury them: God's beautiful creatures.

One night we'd invited the first and second assistant keepers and their wives to our house for an evening of rummy. We wives were having fun beating the men when a loud noise made Elson jump from his chair and go to the window to check the light. Someone said, "It's only a clap of thunder," but Elson started in a hurry for the door, saying, "The birds have struck the tower."

We couldn't believe our eyes as we hustled after him. Hundreds of large birds were everywhere, some injured, some dead, some only dazed. They were brant, a small goose, which must have been migrating south when they were drawn to the light. All of us chased them and caught all we could, as it was almost Thanksgiving and here was an abundant Thanksgiving dinner. Elson and I each caught a brant that was only dazed. The other families preserved all they could for future meals, but we didn't like them for food, so I asked Elson if he would let me put ours in with the hens and tame them. At first he said no, but later gave me permission. The hens didn't seem afraid of them and eventually I tamed them to come to the dish and not hiss at me. I kept them for a while, but they disappeared when we were off Seguin on leave. Luckily, the flock hadn't broken the tower windows or damaged the lens as birds did at Great Duck Island Light.

With two families besides us on Seguin there was much more opportunity to see other people than there had been on Avery. A couple of assistants changed while we were there, so in all there were a number of people. I wasn't as sociable as I should have been, perhaps. I'd been by myself for so long I didn't have that outgoing feeling that I should socialize very much with people. We were friendly with the others, but not very close to them. My ideas and my conceptions were not in common with the others on the light, except for Mrs. Bracy, the first assistant's wife, who was very interested in the education of her children. All of us had much to do, so, except for social occasions like holidays and get-togethers, I didn't spend very much time with the others.

The other wives had large families to care for. Since there were three men to do the work of the station, the women could devote their time to their dwellings and their families. Elson and I didn't have children, and often I'd care for one or another of theirs; I'd frequently make a bed in the big leather chair for baby Jay Bracy, so his mother could tend to her other duties.

There was a child on Seguin whom I thought of adopting, though I had no idea that this would have been possible. A cute little thing, about three years old, she used to come up and stay with me and we'd have a wonderful time. But Elson said adoption wouldn't be advisable. Of course, in those days people felt differently about adopting children not their own. I didn't know just what he thought about it really, because he never went into too much detail about what he felt. He may have been thinking that my health wasn't good enough. I had to rest a lot the first parts of my life, as the peritonitis I'd had when I was two years old affected my ability to do things. I'd had to learn to creep and walk again after the infection passed, and all through school couldn't walk fast like the rest. One high school friend would start earlier for school with me so we could go slowly on the three-mile walk. When we'd play softball, I would pitch and the others would bat and run for me. I've felt far better the latter part of my life than I did in the early years.

We made our own entertainment on Seguin. The tramway had been condemned as unsafe, so a crew of workmen was sent to build a new one. At the same time the machinist, Mr. Fred Morong, came to repair the engines in the whistle house. We knew most of the carpenter crew as they'd been to Avery to repair the boat house and slip. Howard Colbath, the boss carpenter, and Mr. Beal, one of the crew, were from Elson's home town, and Mr. Morong was from mine. Howard played the violin; Elson the banjo, accordion, guitar, and harmonica. I accompanied them on the piano, while Mr. Morong sang along in his nice baritone voice. The Bracy girls, Hilda, Shirley, and Adria, did the Charleston. We had many enjoyable evenings of this type. Mr. Morong was not only a soloist, but a poet also. His poem "Brassworks" celebrated and lamented that unending job of the lightkeeper, polishing brass.

The crew also had wrestling matches. Rough weather had prevented us from getting off Seguin for a time, and our supplies were low. I had just enough meat and potatoes for one meal, stretching it by making a potpie with dumplings. For some reason, I reserved part of the pie when I served it, making the portions smaller and getting comments to that effect. But just before they sat down to the table one of the men grabbed Elson in a wrestling hold, somehow catching his foot. Both landed on the dining room floor with the dishes and food scattered all over them. I knew it was just a spur of-the-moment prank, but I was so provoked, I made them think that all of our food was on the floor. After the innocent ones had chastised the two culprits, I added a few more dumplings to my reserve, opened some canned vegetables, and managed a meal. Elson and his wrestling partner offered their portions to others.

Knee-deep clover and grass covered much of Seguin Island. It was so good to have lawns and a place to plant flowers, not to worry about the hens digging up my plants. Elson built a large, wire enclosure for the chickens where they could scratch and dust their feathers in real dirt.

I soon got over my fear of the snakes on the island as it wasn't long before Kitty found them. He'd had experience with the skates trapped in the gulch at low tide at Avery Rock, dragging them to the house and demanding praise for catching them. On Seguin I soon heard him crying to come in and when I opened the door, found he had a snake he'd bitten so many times it reminded me of a saltshaker. His prize elated him and he expected his customary praise. I took so many away from him, I lost my fear of them. I even got so I could step over a mother snake and her four whitish babies when they persisted in lying in my path to the dump.

The view from our house was particularly beautiful at sunset. Elson's big leather chair just fit in a corner by a west window in the dining room, between the buffet on the north wall and the radio on the west wall. The view of the ocean looked across to Halfway Rock Light Station, Small Point, and Portland Head. I often used this chair. Darning socks was a particular dislike of mine, so I'd cuddle up in this comfortable chair, turn the radio to the ball game or a hockey game, and quickly the socks were wearable again, perfectly darned or Elson wouldn't wear them, because poor darning caused blisters. I knew every player on the ball teams and his record.

Another radio program I listened to was the *Ann Bradford Hour*, a homemaking program. Miss Bradford inquired about featherbeds, so I wrote her, and she wrote me a nice letter back. All of our beds were feather ticks. Elson's father and grandfather were great wild duck hunters and all the downy feathers were saved, cleaned, and used to fill ticking which was placed on top of the regular mattress. We aired the ticks well and often, but they took quite a while to fluff up. When the right height had been obtained by fluffing the tick from underneath with our hands, we used a yardstick, or a broomstick, to smooth the tick. It was so nice looking when properly made. At night you'd sink way down in it, keeping very warm on a cold night.

Another radio show we particularly enjoyed was *Big Brother Bob Emery and His Joy Spreaders*, a program specially produced for the Lighthouse Service and Coast Guard over WEEI in Boston. One of the features of the show was a motorboat trip along the Maine, New Hampshire, and Massachusetts coastline with Big Brother calling on the keepers and Coast Guard men. The sound of the boat seemed just like a real motorboat and we all wondered how they could make the sound in the studio.

We were invited to attend one of the broadcasts, but

Elson couldn't leave the station at that time, so he sent me to represent him. Traveling to Quincy, Massachusetts, I stayed with Elson's sister and joined his brother, Eugene, who took me to the studio. I was lucky to have a seat near Big Brother and his helpers, and saw one of the men begin tapping on a chair whose plywood seat was loose. It was a real surprise; that loose seat sounded like the old Hubbard, make-and-break engine Elson had in one of the boats we'd used for a time at Avery. The trip to the show was a real adventure for me; I still have the pin in the shape of a light bulb representing the station which was sponsored by the Boston Edison Electric Company.

My activities on Seguin included taking cooking lessons by mail from Betty Crocker; I still use the recipes. Reading was also always a favorite of mine, especially historical books. I'd sometimes go to the library at Popham Beach, two miles from the light, but, of course, we also had our library at the light, stocked with donated books and rotated by the Lighthouse Service.

Visitors came to Seguin fairly often. I'd be making my beds when I'd hear a noise and turning, find a group of people at the bedroom door. Because this was a government-owned place, some visitors thought they had a right to go anywhere and do anything and didn't seem to be a bit fazed when I told them this was private, that I did not appreciate people coming in and roaming through my home unless asked. Because we were living on an island, they gave us to understand we were some sort of freaks.

One summer day I had been blueberrying with the Osgoods and their daughter, Leona, the keeper and his family from Perkins Head Light Station up the Kennebec

River. I had about a bushel of beauties I was going to can for winter. The day was beautiful, one of those rare ones when the ocean was calm, the boat lovers taking advantage of it. I could see Portland Head and Small Point from the chair I'd taken out by the back doorstep to watch the boats, some pleasure and some fishing.

I had a quart or so of the berries picked over and was about to winnow another lot by holding the dish full of berries up higher than the pan and letting the breeze blow the leaves and twigs away as the berries fell into the pan below. Just then a monkey came around the corner of the house and jumped right into my big box of berries and began to eat and spit them out. How on earth did a monkey get on Seguin, way out in the ocean? It wasn't long before I had the answer to that. A man came around the house, saw the monkey in the berries, and thinking it was a big joke, called to his friends to come see.

I surely didn't think it was funny and I said to him, "Mister, your monkey has spoiled all my berries I was to can for winter food."

He replied, "Aw, you can use them just the same," and made no apology.

"Perhaps you would use them, but after a monkey has been in the middle of mine as he has been, I wouldn't think of using them." I shall never forget him, for to me he was the freaky one.

Elson was showing a group of visitors around the tower and the man picked up the monkey and started for the tower. I told him he couldn't take the animal up there, as it was against the rules, and that if he went up without it, he would have to wait until the group already up there came down. He allowed he could go up when he wanted to and take the monkey too.

As he started up the winding stairs, the monkey became frightened and began to cry. The cries echoed so loudly in the cylinder, it made him crazy and the man had to let him go. He ran into the first assistant's house attached to ours, where baby Jay was on the floor. The monkey scared poor little Jay almost to death. We were some glad when these visitors left the island.

But most of our visitors were far from unpleasant and my life was changed by one group. If there was no surf or storm, a fleet of gill-netters from Gloucester would anchor near the light. One day, I heard a knock on my porch door. When I opened it, I faced about twenty-five deep-sea gillnetters. Elson, who had seen them from the tower, came to ask what they wanted. I was feeling a little uneasy. To our surprise, they asked if they could come in and listen to an opera that was on the radio that day. Twenty-five men settled in my dining room near the radio, sitting on chairs, sprawling on the floor, anywhere they could hear the music. As I stood in the door looking at this mass of rough-living men, engrossed in the opera, I thought, "Here is an assembly of uncouth sailors with a soul of culture." Until then I had not listened to opera, thinking I'd not enjoy it, but from then on I began to listen to what could hold these men and found I did enjoy it. When the opera ended, they each thanked us and departed as quietly as they had come.

The next day a delegation of three men from the ship came to the door with a sixty-five-pound cod. I just stared at that fish, nearly as large as I was. We thanked them, and as Elson didn't like cod, divided it between the two other families. The keeper with eight children salted some of theirs to have as corned fish with potatoes.

Mr. Law visited us at Seguin, bringing a phonograph

and a dozen records, opera and symphony. He loved them and played them often. I was glad I could share them with him, thanks to the gill-netters.

Mr. Law traveled extensively and wrote of his adventures. These writings, as well as the booklets he sent to his mission, Coast Guard, and lighthouse friends, added up to the hundreds. He would send me proofs of his coming publications because he was always interested in my writing, telling me I must write a book. I saved hundreds of the proofs he sent me up to his death. When it came time for us to leave the light, I thought I wouldn't need these and didn't want to carry them with us, yet I could not burn or destroy them. I cannot explain why, but I gathered them, along with all my letters from my penpals, into a large box lined with oilcloth and buried them there on Seguin. Whether I felt in my subconscious mind that I would go back and get them, or whether I felt I was paying tribute to a good friend, I do not know, but I felt better doing it this way. I often wonder if they are still buried in the same spot and readable. I'd like to have them now.

One morning I was making doughnuts when someone knocked on the door. I opened it to see a lady with the reddest, loveliest hair and nicest smile I'd ever seen. Under her arm were books and papers. "I'm Mrs. Peasley from the Sea Coast Mission. May I come in?"

After I welcomed her she told me, "I have come to ask you to start a Sunday school in the vacant school-house."

"I'm not qualified to do this. I can't."

"Oh yes, you can. We'll help you."

At that time there were about eight or ten children on Seguin old enough to attend, and our Sunday school was a success. One boy, Robert Bracy, then about twelve years old, became very interested and went on to be a minister, teaching in Pennsylvania.

Alice Peasley was so helpful. She even tried to find a market for the quilts I had made and some of the drawings and stories I had done. A few quilts and some studies were sold in New York, before we left Seguin. The drawings were meant for notecards.

Years before we were on Seguin, the government sent schoolteachers out to the lighthouses for a few weeks at a time to teach the children and give instruction and assigned lessons to the parents for the weeks or months until the teachers could return. The last teacher I remember was Lila Severence, who taught my nieces and nephews on Avery Rock and others at the eastern lights of the lighthouse district. Later the teachers were discontinued, and the families went ashore for the school year so the children could go to regular schools. One of the keeper's wives on Seguin spent part of the year on the mainland while her children went to school.

Long after we'd left Seguin, we bought a home in Eliot, Maine. The mailman delivered a package and as I was new to the community, stopped to talk. Imagine my surprise when he told me he had been one of those teachers covering the western lights. His name was Maynard Douglass, who also was one of the soloists in the church I was to attend in Eliot.

Quite often the weather was so bad on Seguin that we couldn't get off to go the two miles to Popham Beach. In the winter of 1930, my father was terminally sick in the hospital in Portsmouth, New Hampshire. I'd been going back and forth from Seguin to Portsmouth for three months and on the seventh of March had just returned from a visit. It was bitter cold and the sea was running high when Elson met me at Popham Beach, icicles hanging from his eyelids and the brim of his sou'wester. We started back to Seguin with the wind blowing heavy and the waves high. The assistant keepers watched us from the tower and later told us that they thought we'd gone to the bottom every time we went deep in a trough. I looked like a polar bear by the time we reached the cove; I didn't want to be under the spray hood so I stood back of the engine box, still getting covered with frozen spray.

We had no telephone service on Seguin, but we were connected to the Coast Guard station at Popham Beach by a cable. The Coast Guard would get messages to us or send them out from us. The phone rang at 2:30 A.M. the next morning. The captain told us that my father had just passed away and they would pick us up later in the morning so we could join the family on the trip to Lubec. A half hour later the cable washed out.

The Coast Guard arrived with the unsinkable lifeboat, the crew wearing life jackets. They put jackets on us and we started out. The captain and Elson were the best of navigators, but I wondered if we would make it as we went through the huge waves breaking all around us as we tried to get to Popham Beach.

Another time the wind at Seguin was so strong we had to get down on our hands and knees and crawl from the brow of the hill to our house. We'd gone to the second assistant's house where the two men did some repair work on the whistle. As we started back up the hill, we realized the wind was blowing exceptionally heavy, but when we came out in the open at the top of the hill we realized just how strong it was. The next morning, the stove began to smoke when we started a fire. Elson went outside to find that all three roofs of the ells on the double dwelling had blown sideways and were nearly on the ground.

Since there were three keepers on Seguin, we did not have to get a substitute whenever we took time off. During a couple of vacations a year, we would take an efficiency apartment at the Eastland Hotel in Portland for fifteen days and go to plays and movies and do a lot of shopping. I particularly loved the arts and crafts departments of the stores, but Elson liked to shop too. We had friends on Peaks Island, just off Portland, whom we liked to visit.

One winter was very rugged, and nerves were very touchy. Long spells of damp weather and fog had caused problems with the whistle, so Elson had been working hard to repair the engine and keep it running until the machinist could come and do the overhauling in a few weeks.

The kitchen door slammed. Elson went directly to the telephone to call the District Office for a leave of absence. Then he came over and put his arms around me, saying, "I've had it. We're taking a three-day leave of absence. Get your bag packed, find the sterno stove, and bundle up some blankets. We'll go to Bath and stay aboard the boat at the pier."

I had molasses cookies rolled out on the breadboard ready to bake, so I put them in the oven, trying at the same time to pack food, blankets, checkerboard, and warm clothing. A winter chill was in the April air. Drifting ice filled the Kennebec as the inlets shed their winter coats. As we sailed out of Seguin cove this beautiful day, I could see Elson relax and knew this was what he needed.

The little sterno stove kept us dry and warm, despite there being no cabin on the boat, but only the long spray hood. We caught fish over the side of the boat and cooked them over the sterno stove. When the smell of fresh fish filled the air, we welcomed visitors from the Popham mail boat docked nearby aboard to share. We had so much fun those three days. It ended all too soon.

Casting off the line the third day, we backed out into the river, our engine purring. We breathed in the fresh air as we sailed along at a good speed in the ice-free channel while on each side of the channel, small and large squares of ice, covered with sticks, grass, and rock-weed, floated. Passing Doubling Point Light, we could see several boats coming toward Bath, including the Popham Beach mail steamer.

I wondered why Elson suddenly slowed the engine. Then he said, "Connie, that is a body floating by the mail boat."

I looked and said, "No Elson, it's a barrel."

But he was sure. "I've seen too many when I was on the ship during the war to mistake it." He headed the boat toward the object. Coming alongside, he took the gaff and touched the shape; the body came up.

"Take the tiller, Connie, and steer the boat. I've got somehow to get this body to land."

The law forbid taking a body aboard our boat, so Elson had to tend to the body while we towed it.

Afraid it would come apart, he wrapped it cradlelike in rope. The engine was slowed as low as possible, but even at this speed it wasn't easy for me to manage a forty-five-foot powerboat in ice and swift tide, though somehow I did. Neither of us spoke and once in a while Elson would look away from the body long enough to see if I was on course.

It was quite a distance to the lighthouse opposite Phippsburg, the nearest town. "Steer for the light, Connie. I'll put you ashore to stay with the keeper and his family until I get back from Phippsburg." I didn't realize

I'd had any reaction to all this until I stepped out onto the slip and found my legs were shaking. I was afraid for Elson to go alone, but he insisted I stay there.

He went to a mansion across the river from the light to use the telephone to call the authorities. The lady at the house told him she'd read a while ago that a lady in Hallowell had offered a reward for any information about her husband, who had been missing since December. He'd owned an electrical business located on the wharf in Hallowell, and during an ice storm with an exceptionally high tide, had gone to the wharf to check his store. She hadn't seen him since. Further, he was wearing glasses, a mackinaw, a gold ring with the initial "A," and was lame in one knee.

Except for the glasses, the body matched this description. Soon the police, undertaker, and the usual curious gathering were helping to take care of the body, which was in excellent condition because it had been frozen in the ice all this time.

After we got over the shock of finding the body, we thought how fortunate it was that it had stayed in the main current of the river rather than go into Merrymeeting Bay, where it wouldn't have been found until much later when duck hunters used the bay. The mail boat and several other smaller boats had passed it by just that day, thinking like I did that it was a barrel, not recognizing it as a person. Had Elson not seen it, it would have gone with the current out to sea.

We had a letter from the man's wife, Mrs. Aldridge, offering Elson a reward of one hundred dollars. He wouldn't take it, telling her to give it to her church or to charity if she couldn't use it, but she had an aged mother to take care of and could use the money. She wrote, "We prayed every day for some news of my husband and cannot tell you how much we appreciated your finding him."

It was a tragic experience, but we both felt such peace that God could give this lady the comfort she had prayed for, and we were His helpers.

Another leave to Bath almost didn't happen: we were lucky not to be in quarantine. The second assistant came to our house one night, insisting that I go to take his wife's temperature. As wife of the head keeper, I was in charge of the medicine box, and the others often came to me when there was sickness. I thought the woman was going to chew up the thermometer, her teeth were chattering so. The mercury showed a temperature of 104 degrees plus. We had the Coast Guard put through a call to a doctor friend of ours who, on hearing the temperature, thought I'd made a mistake reading it. He told me he'd call me at six o'clock the next morning. If the temperature was the same, he'd come out. It cost so much, we only had doctors come out to Seguin when absolutely necessary.

I stayed with the woman that night to tend to her and to her small baby, while her husband tended the other children. She was delirious and very, very ill. The next morning the temperature still registered at 104 degrees so the doctor came out. His thermometer showed 104 and eight-tenths degrees and he diagnosed typhoid fever. He ordered her to the hospital in Bath. Now, how were we to get her there safely?

I had a new, warm flannel nightdress that we put on her, along with heavy socks. A stretcher was made and I told the others to heat bricks, which I placed along her sides, remembering this from my bout with pneumonia. The doctor was pleased and surprised, wondering how I knew to do this, and ordered only another blanket. In the dead of winter she was taken in an open boat the sixteen miles to Bath.

The light was quarantined and fumigated, but no one else contracted the typhoid, the source of which we never knew for sure. The sick woman later recovered. The doctor said that Elson and I could go on our leave, which we had planned, as long as we were under the supervision of a doctor in Bath. The leave started out with the roughest trip I can remember, so rough I got down and prayed. I never doubted Elson's navigational skills, but was afraid the rope on the tiller would break and we'd be at the mercy of the waves coming at us in all directions. We did make it and enjoyed the time away from the light.

In time Seguin began to be old hat for us, so Elson asked to be considered for the Saint Croix River Light Station, known locally as Dochet Island, or simply, Dochet's. Situated in the Saint Croix River, half a mile from Red Beach, Ward Seven of Calais, Maine, and half a mile from the Canadian shore, just above Saint Andrews, New Brunswick, this was a single-family station and much nearer than Seguin to both Elson's family and mine. We were notified that a vacancy would occur in September 1930, and on September 23 we left Seguin in fog and rain. We'd had a happy reunion with Captain Faulkingham, the mate, and crew who had landed us on Seguin four years before. Kitty was not traveling with us on this move; he had taken sick and died on Seguin. Our furniture was covered and strapped safely on the rear deck. Our forty-five-foot powerboat was lifted as easily as though it were a rowboat and lashed to the deck. The fog shut in thick.

I stood waving to the families we were sorry to leave and to our lighthouse home of four years with its good memories and a few sorrows. We'd met many interesting people we liked and some we didn't enjoy. I gave a final wave to those dear people we'd shared the light with and turned to enter the stateroom, feeling a little sadness, but also the excitement of starting a new journey to a strange place. I'd be starting a new life and home, but one near my hometown, and near my mother, sisters, and brothers. Though I tried to think of pleasant things or the past as future, but at the slightest scraping of the hull the image of a big hole would yawn in my mind. I'd miss my dear father who had passed away the March before.

The tender headed for the Cuckold's Light, by Boothbay Harbor and Ram Island, piloting through a heavy fog and wind. There were many ledges in this course, and the passageway was narrow. The captain was trying to run for the bell buoy, but the wind was taking the sound away from us. This passage was so treacherous, he had slowed the engines; you could hear a pin drop and feel the tension. Time seemed to slow down as the boat edged forward. Finally, right on course, the watch said, "There it is on our port side." What welcome words! We really sighed with relief.

The foul weather lasted until we docked in Rockland. There, the mate invited us to go to a movie. We returned aboard about 10:30 P.M., tired, since we'd been on the go since 4:30 that morning.

When we got up at sunrise, the tender was being readied to leave. Our next stop was Heron Neck Light Station, where we picked up the keeper and his family and possessions and took them to Southwest Harbor where he planned to retire. His wife and son came on board, the son carrying a Pekingese under each arm. They couldn't be allowed to run on deck, so they stayed under his arms all across Penobscot Bay, barking all the way.

After dropping off these passengers, we headed to Isle au Haut to pump fresh water to carry to the cisterns at the lighthouse. Rain had been scarce and the cisterns were dry, leaving the keeper without drinking water.

When we passed Libby Island Light, I went out on deck and looked up Machias Bay trying to see Avery Rock, but it was just a speck in the distance.

As we neared Lubec I relived moments from my childhood there: Peacock's Canning Company and the Lubec waterfront; one of the houses we'd lived in up on the hill; the bandstand and park where, dressed in red, white, or blue, we'd formed a giant American flag during the 100th celebration; Friar's Head Rock that had loomed out of the fog the day my father took Gerald and me on the Lubec ferry to Welch Pool, Campobello, where other Lubeckers had gathered for a picnic; the high bank in Lubec from which we'd looked down on the American Can plant where the still-healthy Franklin Roosevelt would tie his boat to the wharf and talk to the men.

We arrived in Lubec Channel at 3 A.M. Excited over my return to native surroundings, I peered out the porthole to see Channel Light still flashing. It was a calm, dark morning, everything asleep along the shore. Slipping my coat on, I stepped out on the deck where I could smell the flats and draw in the fresh salt air. Captain Faulkingham came down from the pilothouse and joined me. For a few minutes we both enjoyed the still peace, broken only by the churning of the engines and the turning of the rudder.

He asked me if I was glad to be Downeast again and if I'd be lonesome on our new home, after Seguin. I assured him that after the four years on Avery Rock, I was certain this would be heaven.

I asked him why we were sailing at this hour. "On account of the tide," he answered. "We have to make nearly high tide on the Saint Croix to land your furniture and household effects. We also have the yearly supply of coal on board."

We were by this time approaching the narrows between Lubec and Campobello Island, so Captain Faulkingham returned to the pilothouse. After a few minutes, I went back to our stateroom. My husband still slept, getting his rest for this first day of our new life.

SIX

SAINT CROIX, OR DOCHET'S, ISLAND

I wondered if Saint Croix Island had been as beautiful to Sieur de Monts and Samuel de Champlain in 1604 as it was to me now. Saint Andrews, New Brunswick, was to the starboard as we went through the calm waters of Saint Andrews Bay into the Saint Croix River. It was just before dawn and the occasional bark of a dog or crow of a rooster echoed across the still water.

Elson and I went into the pilothouse where Captain Faulkingham pointed out Perry; the Passamaquoddy Indian reservation; and Bunker Point, half in Robbinston and half in the town of Red Beach, named for its red granite and gravel. All along the Canadian or eastern shore were farms where we later bought vegetables and strawberries.

We came abreast of our island as the sun came up over the Canadian mountains. The keeper, Captain Kinney, was just extinguishing the light, arranging the cover, and drawing the shades. The tender anchored and the crew quickly filled the supply boat on the first of its many trips to the island with our belongings.

The house was empty except for the three orange crates Captain Kinney used for furniture after his possessions had been moved to Machias, where he and Mrs. Kinney were retiring. Our voices echoed in the empty rooms until our furniture began filling them. Three large bedrooms, a living room, a dining room, a kitchen, a back entry, a rotting piazza we would make into a comfortable sun parlor, and a large basement made up the house. As on Avery Rock, the tower, here octagonal, was built on top of the house, so visitors had to go through the house to get to it.

By afternoon the tender had left. At two o'clock I was washing cupboards and unpacking dishes and trying to organize them, when Elson came in from his outside work. He had a habit of dropping his chin down and looking at me intently over his glasses. I turned as he was doing this. I'd been so busy I didn't realize my face and arms were streaked with dust and the ends of my hair, which was long and worn in a coil at the back, had escaped from its pins. I thought, "What have I done?"

He was so serious, but then a gleam came into his eyes. "You are a mess."

"Elson Small, if you say one word more, I'll cry."

He put his hands on my shoulders, and when I looked up at him, I saw that he was happy. He was never demonstrative, though I knew he loved me, so he surprised me by holding me tight to him and saying, "You may look a mess, but you look so good to me. I've come in to ask you to take a walk with me around the island."

So, hand in hand, we covered every inch of our new home, realizing as we went that it was a little paradise. Already Elson had plans to buy a cow for fresh milk, to buy some kind of machinery to plant a garden, to order a few chickens, and to sell our forty-five-foot motorboat because it was too big for our use here. The Saint Croix River was calm after Avery Rock and Seguin and the distance to either the Canadian or American shore was only half a mile.

Besides the dwelling, a bell tower, boat house, barn, oil house, and utility building were constructed on the lighthouse grounds. Elson later built a workshop on the privately owned land adjoining the government land.

We went down to the two lovely beaches and walked along the edge of the water, throwing rocks and listening to them plop in the river. As the water ebbed we discovered we could dig clams — lots of them. Climbing over the rocks beyond the beach, we saw goose tongue greens, which I used to gather in Lubec. So there were two sources of food. Then we saw a third: black ducks, coots, and whistlers offshore. We were indeed in paradise.

Coming back up the bank, Elson challenged me to the first of many races to the house. I never won any of these races, but they were invigorating. By the time we reached the house, we both felt it was time to relax. I had been awake since 3 A.M. and he almost as long. Thus, our first day passed, and we both were well satisfied.

Dochet's was a small island, the main part about five acres in all. The light sat on the highest section, a rock ledge about fifty-two feet above extreme high tide, about sixty-two feet above mean tide level. Just below the lighthouse a fence divided the land owned by the government from the privately owned section where we pastured our cow and planted our vegetable gardens, and where Elson had the workshop. The land on the west side of the island sloped, leveling off to the edge of the river where the boat house was built, while the entire east side was a bluff, thirty-five or forty feet high, lined with trees. The deepest water was on the east side of the island and this channel formed the boundary line between the United States and Canada, giving the island to the United States.

The south end of the island sloped to the water, forming a sandbank which attracted many visitors for the fun of sliding down it to the beach below. When we first went to Dochet's, a wooden fence fortified a bar connecting two nubbles which had been part of the main island during Champlain's time. By the time we left in sixteen years, the bar had eroded away and the river flowed over it in extreme high water. Between the sandbank and nubbles was the cove where we beached our boats and had picnics and bonfires, roasting corn, lobsters, and clams.

A hay field covered the north end, the red oil house in its center. Aside from the ledge the house sat on, there was only one other rock on the island, a large granite bolder to which a plaque had been fastened in commemoration of the discovery of Saint Croix Island by Sieur de Monts and Champlain.

By the early part of the year 1604 not a single European had settled the northern part of North America. A few attempts had been made but were unsuccessful. The very country was in dispute; both England and France claimed it. At about this time, Sieur de Monts, a prominent soldier and gentleman of France, asked the king if he might establish a colony in Acadia. He was willing to finance the expedition on the condition that he be given the monopoly for the fur trade. Not only was this readily granted, but de Monts was also made lieutenant general for the country of Acadia, which at that time reached from Philadelphia to Cape Breton.

Sieur de Monts gathered together a band of about 120 men: some gentlemen in search of adventure, some artisans, and some workmen. With plenty of supplies to make a permanent settlement, they set sail in two ships: one a vessel of 129 tons, the other 159 tons. With them was the king's geographer, Samuel de Champlain. The ships reached Acadia safely in May, and on June 16, Sieur de Monts and Champlain, taking a small boat of about eight tons, began their explorations of the Bay of Fundy, entering the mouth of the Saint John on June 24. From there they went westward by the islands now known as the Wolves, into Passamaquoddy Bay and on up the river.

As Champlain wrote: "We entered a river almost half a league in breadth at its mouth, sailing up which a league or two we found two islands, one very small near the western bank, and the other in mid-river, having a circumference of perhaps eight or nine hundred paces, with rocky sides three or four fathoms high all around, except in one small place, where there is a sandy point and clayey earth adapted for making brick and other needful articles. There is another place affording a shelter for vessels from eighty to a hundred tons, but it is dry at low tide. The island is covered with firs, birches, maples and oaks. It is by nature very well situated, except in one place, where for about forty paces it is lower than elsewhere; this, however, is easily fortified. The banks of the mainland are distant on both sides some nine hundred to a thousand paces. Vessels could pass up the river only at the mercy of the cannon on this island, and we deemed the location the most advantageous not only on account of its situation and good soil, but also on account of the intercourse which we proposed with the Indians of these coasts and the interior, as we should be in the midst of them. We hoped to pacify them in the course of time and put an end to the wars which they carry on with one another, so as to derive service from them in the future, and convert them to the Christian faith. This place was named by Sieur de Monts Saint Croix Island."

Champlain was quoted by Professor Ganong in an address given at the Tercentenary of de Monts' Settlement at Saint Croix Island, on June 25, 1904, and published in 1905 by the Maine Historical Society. This discovery did not go forgotten!

The settlers began building houses and planting gardens, but rain was scarce, and in the sandy loam of the island, the crops dried up. The winter of 1604 came early and the river froze over. The settlers, having no fresh water, drank snow water. Their diet consisted mostly of salt meat. Thirty-five died of scurvy and were buried on the southern end of the island, which has since eroded away.

In time the settlers built twelve buildings on Saint Croix Island, all of which were destroyed in 1613 in an attack by the English Captain Samuel Argall of Virginia.

The history of the island has been of great interest to many. While we were there, people wrote for souvenirs of this first settlement north of Florida, and visitors to the area searched for evidence of the early settlement.

One day some summer visitors playing on the sandbank uncovered the end of a box that looked like it contained a casket. Scared and excited, they came running up to the house to see if Elson would investigate. Elson decided the box was too small to hold a man's body. He didn't disturb it, but contacted the proper authorities who found that it contained the body of a dog, which turned out to be the pet dog of a former lighthouse keeper. It was claimed by the owner and placed in another resting place. The summer visitors were disappointed, for they thought surely they had found one of Champlain's men.

In 1949, after we had left the island, President Truman signed a bill authorizing a national monument on Saint Croix Island commemorating the first French settlement in North America. Work was still being done in October 1976, the house scheduled to become a museum, when vandals rowed to the island and built a fire in the wooden bell house during a fifty-mile-an-hour wind, burning all of the buildings except the boat house. A big loss to both the United States and Canada!

Our first Christmas on Dochet's it snowed hard. In the three months we'd been there I hadn't met our neighbors on the mainland; I'd been a homebody except for the couple of times I'd gone ashore to the post office. For Christmas dinner I baked a chicken with all the fixings and set the table with the china and silver we'd bought for our new home. I thought my table looked very festive and hoped it would bring joy to my husband.

I had learned that the first Christmas in North America had been celebrated here. Going to the window, I looked out at the big flakes silently falling as if they were trying to spread a white mantle in honor of the birth of our Lord. I thought of Champlain and de Monts and their 120 men, wondering how they had celebrated the day. In the group were a Roman Catholic priest and a Protestant minister, and the first community church in North America was here. The clergymen had both died during that first, rugged winter. Since they had argued through all the days they were together, the settlers buried them in a single grave on the southern part of the island, hoping they would be at peace with each other from then on.

I felt rich with a good husband, good food, my canary

Peter, my cat Topsy, and the spirits of those brave men of the early settlement. I only wished I could share my dinner with those less fortunate. After dinner Elson played the banjo as I accompanied him on the piano, playing Christmas music we loved, ending the day feeling it had been quite beautiful.

Later, another Christmas as exciting as Dochet's was drawn into history. December 9, 1941, dawned cold, but sunny. Patches of snow lay here and there on the island and the mainland. There was no ice on the river; the water was calm. Elson was repairing a frayed winch rope when I saw the flag signal at the boat landing at Red Beach go up. I went down to tell Elson someone was signaling him to come ashore after them. Taking the rowboat with the outboard attached, he went ashore.

There he found Mr. John Trimble and Mr. Arthur Unobsky, two businessmen from Calais, and a Mr. Earl Doucette. Elson knew Mr. Trimble and Mr. Unobsky real well, but Mr. Doucette, who was carrying camera equipment, was a stranger. They asked Elson if he would help to add to a historical event.

Mr. Trimble and Mr. Unobsky represented the Calais Chamber of Commerce. They introduced Mr. Doucette as the representative of the publicity bureau of the state government in Augusta. Pearl Harbor had just been attacked and it had been decided to send a Christmas tree from the site of the first Christmas celebrated in North America to the White House in Washington, where President Roosevelt was entertaining Mr. Winston Churchill for Christmas.

A beautifully shaped tree, about eighteen feet high, and one of a very few left on the island, was chosen. If it hadn't been for a historical purpose, I would have felt quite bad to have it cut down. Mr. Doucette was to take movies and pictures for the archives in the State House in Augusta. He took several pictures of the men as they decided how many limbs to remove before cutting the tree down, but before he could get his movie equipment ready, Elson had chopped the tree to the moment it would fall. Fall it started to do, and Mr. Doucette began to holler, "Push it back up! I want to get movies of its falling!" So, the men, with all the brawn and muscle they could muster, pushed the tree back and then let it fall in its graceful way.

Mr. Unobsky was quite a stout gentleman. He gave us a good demonstration of how fast a short, heavy man could run when he saw the tree coming down and thought it was going to hit him. They were all good sports and it was a great event.

Elson had to tie up this large tree, get it aboard his boat and the nine miles to Calais, to ship it by train from Calais to Washington. His comment: "It was quite an undertaking, but I was glad to contribute to history."

After our time on Seguin with its huge first order light, the fifth order light on Dochet's was small. The old kerosene wick lamp had been replaced by an Aladdin lamp with a mantle which required a small pump to create pressure to make the kerosene vaporize before the mantle turned white with heat. However, the lamp smoked up very quickly if not properly lighted, necessitating a massive cleanup job to get rid of the greasy soot.

To any keeper the tower and lamp was his baby, and he tended and cared for it with as much attention. To Elson, of course, this care extended to everything on the island. He bought firewood for the summer kitchen stove, and stacked it in neat tiers in the basement. Not only was the wood swept clean, but the floor underneath was painted and shellacked. Even the hen pen was as clean as possible and the hens very well cared for. I once heard him tell a friend that his hens sang the best opera he ever heard. The hen pen windows even had awnings to keep the pen cool.

Elson's ways might lead one to think he was an old fuddy-duddy, but he wasn't. He had a manner of accomplishing this order by making it fun and a source of pride, so that everyone wanted to help. Our relationship was comradely; we both felt such satisfaction when all was proper at the unannounced lighthouse inspections.

The bell tower at Dochet's was near the water on the channel side. It was built in a tall pyramid shape with the bell fastened to a framework outside, over the water. We operated the machinery by winding weights by winch to the top of the tower. As the bell struck, a weight would fall a certain distance. A clock on the machinery timed the strokes of the hammer to hit the bell. From the top of the tower it was a long drop to the rocks below the bank; I always held my breath when Elson hoisted himself up with blocks to paint the tower.

If there was fog or thick snow, navigators would run for the bell. Even if the night was clear when we went to bed, we often would wake with a start and could feel the fog coming in. Elson would go to the bell tower and start the bell.

Heavy fog was frequent on Dochet's. Once, at 4:00 A.M. we were sound asleep when a pounding came on the door. Elson bounded out of bed, thinking something was wrong with the light or fog bell, but it was two sailors who had been lost in the week of fog we had been having. Somehow they had missed all the land and islands from the Bay of Fundy where they went to trawl for fish and had hit the sandbar on the back side of our island.

Their boat had had engine trouble and they drifted two days before they got the engine working. Planning to be gone one day, they had taken no extra food, so had gone hungry for two days and were famished. Elson called me to get together some food for them while he went out to milk the cow. I baked a pan of hot biscuits, cooked bacon, boiled eggs, and put it all in a big pan together with homemade preserves for them to take back aboard their boat.

About eleven o'clock the next morning the men came back, bringing our milk pail full of scallops. They had discovered a small bed just to the north of the island. One sat down in my kitchen chair and said, "You have saved our lives. That milk was so good we drunk it right down."

Our years on Dochet's took on a pattern. In the summers we saw a lot of people and did a lot with them, purposely saving what tasks we could for the winter. In September the summer cottages were closed up for the winter. From October to April we saw very few visitors and we settled down to the repair work on the station, painting the interior of the buildings and generally getting the station ready for spring inspection. Winter was a time for me to do my quilts and new tidies for chairs and tables. I started making a quilt with embroidered squares and decided to design one that told the story of our life on the island. Drawing pictures of particular events on unbleached cotton, I embroidered them in outline with a few solid places of embroidery. One winter I also hemstitched five pair of pongee curtains for the bay window in the dining room. Done with double row and crossover stitch, they were a lot of work.

Besides the work he did on the station, Elson built boats during the winter. This work really started with a visit from my brother Gerald and his wife, Grace. They started visiting us weekends while Gerald was principal of the Calais Junior High School for a time. The first visit was on a cold weekend, the weather poor. Every few moments I went to the window to look at the landing in Red Beach. Finally I saw their car, so Elson put on his heavy clothing and went to the boat house to launch his outboard for the short trip over the choppy water. I watched Gerald and Grace walk to the point to meet Elson, then I put on my own jacket to go help them at the slip.

We had a nice reunion as we hadn't seen them for a long time. Grace and I spent the time in the house, cooking and sewing. Grace loved to cook and helped me with the meals. We had a wonderful time together. Later, Gerald and Grace also became summer visitors as they would substitute for us when we went on our fifteen-day vacation. It made a nice vacation for them and their children, though. Once Gerald was there alone and said that at first it would be ten o'clock at night before he could get all the chores done. I don't think he'd ever milked a cow before and I'm sure had never washed a cream separator.

At the time of the first weekend visit, Elson's dinghy was ready for the scrap pile so Gerald brought an armload of *Popular Mechanics* magazines. He and Elson were going to build a boat. They went down to the workshop in the pasture, made a fire in the woodstove, and proceeded to draft a model of a speedboat which they continued to work on over the months.

The speedboat proved such a success and Elson was so encouraged, he started building rowboats for himself. They were beautiful and better still, very seaworthy. He would build a fire in the woodstove in the workshop and spend much of the day building. On those cold, snowy days when we couldn't get out to do much exercise, I'd pack a lunch and go down to help him. My usual job was to hold the iron against the wood while he clinched the nails into the plank.

Elson and Gerald got their heads together again and built a windmill which worked perfectly to solve our problem of getting power. As we had no electricity on the island, everything that used power had to be operated by storage batteries. It was quite a job to get them ashore, so Elson's and Gerald's windmill saved us that.

One summer day a yacht sailed by the light, then suddenly turned, came back, and anchored in the cove. A nice-looking gentleman dressed in yachting clothes came up to the windmill and asked Elson who made it. When he was told "my brother-in-law and myself," he told Elson to have it patented right away. We soon discovered that he was Mr. Gano Dunn, of the White Engineering Corporation of New York. Unfortunately, Elson didn't patent the windmill, and two years later these windmills began to appear on the market.

While we were on Dochet's I gave up my painting. The desire to paint had never left me, and it surfaced often. Not having one room or a studio, I painted anywhere, on the floor, in our bedroom, in the dining room. Sometimes I would paint because I was frustrated. One such instance was my reaction to the chore of painting the long, white fence around the dwelling on Dochet's. I hated painting that fence but it had to be done. The chosen day was a gorgeous summer one. Everyone else was in boats or on the shore having a wonderful time and I desperately wanted to be doing something, anything, else. Finally, I stopped. I got a canvas-covered board and with lamp black, burnt umber, chrome green, yellow ochre, and red lead, using the small brush I used to paint the fence posts with red lead, I painted a picture of the dwelling and long, white fence. Then I lay down for a while. When I got up all my dissatisfied feelings had gone because I had done something different. I call the painting "My Rebellion."

Usually when I was painting pictures I got so engrossed that time did not exist for me, and before I knew it Elson was coming in for a dinner that was not ready. When a person loves something the way I loved painting, nothing else penetrates, and I knew that neglecting Elson would happen too many times. That wouldn't have been right, so I thought I might as well put the painting away right then until the time came when I could take it out again. He worked hard and came in expecting something to eat so he could get back to his work again. It wasn't very satisfactory for him not to be able to depend on that and I wasn't going to let it happen, so I laid away something I loved. In my mind I knew I'd have to choose and I did and it was the right thing to do at the time. Perhaps Grandmother's words about sacrifice, so many years ago, had been a seed sown in my mind.

I think the reason Elson and I were so close and so happy was that I put inside of me my desires, my long- ings, things I wanted to do, if they came in conflict with what he wanted. I felt what I wanted were selfish desires. I knew later they weren't selfish, but I didn't think so then and one or the other had to give, so I gave and I've never been sorry. He was a very set person, if he said no, he meant no, and usually you couldn't change him. I would say no, but others could convince me to say yes. It wasn't easy. I wanted to rebel, desperately so at times, but I didn't.

I filled my life with Elson and that's how we got along. I'd be so busy making it work and doing things he wanted me to do, like shooting pistols and accompanying him on the piano — things I wouldn't have done without his encouragement — I forgot to be unhappy and I found joy. In turn, he would sometimes surprise me by suggesting we do things I liked.

I never really got mad at Elson. My feelings were hurt very deeply at times, or I felt he could have been more considerate, but I never showed it except to say, "I don't think that's right," or "I'm not happy with that." Sometimes, when he'd get mad at me, he'd take the boat and go ashore or he'd go to his workshop. Later he'd come back and we'd sit down and talk the problem over. That was it. It was solved, not thought of again. Sometimes he would consider my way and change his idea. We never really quarreled. We had our differences.

Elson and I were almost always together. Even on Dochet's where we had more opportunity than at the other lights to see other people or do other things, he wanted me to wait on him or to be with him. If he just went down to the garden and I wasn't doing anything in the house, he wanted me with him.

Elson and I had fun together. One winter it was twenty-seven below zero for over two weeks. The river froze solid. We wrapped up the cow in one of our best wool blankets for fear she would freeze. We couldn't do much except make sure the water pipes and cisterns didn't freeze, keep the slip clear of ice, and repair the damage caused by snow and sleet.

I had learned to target shoot with Elson's encouragement. He was an excellent target shooter, having learned as a small boy when Billy Hill, a trick shot and a salesman and demonstrator for the Remington Rifle

Company, stayed with the Smalls at Cross Island Coast Guard Station. Mr. Hill had taught Elson to throw walnuts, cans, and other objects into the air and break them before they reached the ground. On Dochet's, Elson wanted me to learn to shoot so we could both compete at the Rod and Gun Club field days. We practiced often and I could shoot well enough to make it interesting for Elson. In fact, at the field days we usually came in first and second in target shooting competitions.

During the freeze-in we would go down to the shore and shoot icicles just to get the fresh air and exercise. The warm kitchen always felt so good when we came back. One of these frozen days, when fresh food was low, Elson went down to the shore hoping he would get a few clams, but about six feet of ice covered the beach, so clamming was impossible. As he started for the house he noticed a flopping out a short distance in one of the holes full of water left by the ebbing tide and saw that a fish had been caught there. For fear it would get away, he fired a shot at it and knew he had hit it.

He later told me he hollered to me to bring his hip boots, but I was way up at the house and couldn't hear him. I looked out of the window and saw him coming, soaking wet and freezing, and hurried to see what had happened. He came in and laid a haddock in the sink. It weighed about six pounds, a beauty. He had tried to make me hear, but afraid he'd lose the fish, had waded out up above his knees with just his overshoes on. Sure enough, there was a bullet hole right through the fish's head.

Because the tide rose and fell twenty-five feet, Elson thought it unsafe to go out on the frozen river. But after we'd been frozen in for two weeks our food was low, so we walked down to the boat house for Elson to test the safety of the ice. About a mile upriver a span of horses and a sled crossed from the Canadian shore to Devil's Head on the Calais side. Elson worked his way out on the ice by the boat house, chopped down eighteen inches and didn't see water, so he said, "Put your things on, we're going to walk ashore." He tied the ends of a rope about twenty-five feet long to each of us in case one fell into an air hole. We took poles and poled ourselves down onto the ice below.

Our snowshoes were strapped on our backs. Once on the ice, we put them on and snowshoed to the highway, then walked to the post office. A pair of hunting boots I had ordered from Sears, Roebuck had come that day, so I sat down in the middle of the Saint Croix River and put them on. I expect I am the only person to change her shoes in the Saint Croix River and keep dry.

Summers on Dochet Island were busy with tourists and friends. As spring came, the martins returned to the birdhouse Elson had built for them. A little later, the cottages on both sides of the river came to life and the river itself filled with yachts and boats of all kinds. The Grand Manan steamer passed by on her way to Saint Stephen. Passamaquoddy Indians paddled by in straight lines on their way to pick sweet grass or capture seals.

Elson was out in our forty-five-foot Jonesport one day, readying her to sell for a smaller boat, when he saw a Jonesport cabin cruiser, the *Madkath,* coming over from Bunker Point. He was challenged to a race and that is how we became friends with the captain of the cruiser, Dr. Willard Bunker of Calais, owner of Bunker Point, where he and his wife, Kate, and family had a cottage. Aboard was his eight-year-old daughter Ruth, who became like a daughter to us. She and Elson spent many hours talking and running boats. When she and her sisters, Madeline and Katherine, had their own sailboat, she and Elson would race it in the yacht club regatta at Bunker Point.

One early summer day, Ruth rowed over to Dochet's in her peanut shell to invite us to a picnic dinner. Doctor was going to launch his cabin cruiser that day, but he and Packy, his caretaker, decided it was too big a job for two men. Other guests began to arrive for the picnic, first one, then another giving Doctor instructions on launching the boat. No one but Elson actually knew much about boats and there was much merriment and friendship as the women got things ready for the chowder.

All seemed to be going fine until the wedge holding the *Madkath* was knocked away to allow the boat to slide into the water. Suddenly, a board somehow came loose and pinned Doctor's leg. No one moved but Elson, who dashed to get the leg clear. Doctor insisted he was all right and that they should finish the launching. The boat slipped into the river in a graceful way, but the men soon realized that she was leaking badly, more than would be usual from seams that had dried up and shrunk over the winter. They decided to beach her on Dochet's to see where the leak was. Elson went ahead in his boat and by the time the *Madkath* reached the island, the water was coming in so fast the men had to pump with all their might. As the tide was half down, they left her until the tide was low, Elson offering to watch her.

After Elson finished his station work he checked on the boat. The others hadn't realized just how fast she had been taking in water, and he came running up for me to go down and bail while he went for Doctor Bunker. The water was up to the floor and still rising. I hopped aboard and bailed as fast as I could until I was half-exhausted and felt I couldn't do any more. Then I'd realize that if I stopped, the water would come up over the engine and ruin that, and I'd bail all the harder. It was a losing battle, for as fast as I threw one pailful over, it would be right back in.

Elson had taken the speedboat, so it wasn't long before Doctor and his brother-in-law, Hadley Weeks, were there. We all bailed and pumped until the water was down to the keel, where we finally found the cause of the leak. Much to everyone's embarrassment, the plug that had been removed in the fall to let water out of the boat when she was hauled up for the winter had not been replaced. The plug in, the tide floated the *Madkath* and there were no leaks.

We had much fun on the *Madkath* with the Bunkers. On a trip from Calais to Camden in the middle of the Maine coast, we decided to stay in Bucksport overnight. A strong tide ran through the section of the Penobscot River we took to Bucksport. Doctor and Elson were in the pilothouse. Sitting on top of the pilothouse, I was enjoying the beautiful day and scenery. Kate was on the deck below me. Suddenly, the engine stopped short and the tide was fast taking us toward the pier. Elson was so quick it seemed his feet didn't touch the deck as he moved from bow to stern, calling to Kate and me to get down in the bottom of the boat quick, cutting the painter to the dinghy we were towing. The painter had caught around the shaft and propeller, stopping the engine, rendering the rudder helpless.

At that moment *Madkath* struck the pier, going under it, taking the flag and for a few minutes we thought the pilothouse. But she was stopped by a protruding spike that punched a hole in the bow. After we examined the hole, we went into the galley expecting that we would have lost our dinner of beans baking in the galley stove, that they would have spilled all over. But we found the bean pot teetering on the edge of the oven and rescued it, our Saturday night supper intact.

Elson and Doctor went ashore in Bucksport to buy some tools, a plank board, and some paint. From a standing position in the dinghy, Elson repaired the hole in the bow so well no one could notice where the boat had been damaged. We decided that Elson was as expert mending damage to a boat as Doctor was repairing the human body. That was a great compliment, for Doctor was an excellent surgeon.

The next morning we continued up the Penobscot to Bangor where the Bunkers' daughter, Madeline, came aboard for a visit. Doctor decided he would have to put the *Madkath* in dry dock to have the shaft straightened, so we sailed down to Camden, the nearest place to have it done. While the men supervised the work, Kate and I visited the amphitheater, a beautiful spot given to the town of Camden by Mr. Cyrus Curtis, of the Curtis Publishing Company, who was a summer resident.

As we returned down the coast, our food supply got low. Doctor said he knew where we could find clams and goose tongue greens, and we headed for this cove. The fog had set in thick, the sea was rough, so after we got our clams and greens, we decided that it wasn't a good place to lay out a storm so we headed for a nearby harbor. The passageway was narrow with ledges everywhere — the kind of waterway that always made me most nervous. Kate was nervous too. Not to let her know how nervous I was and upset her more, I began to pack and unpack my suitcase, again and again. Doctor, noticing, said, "Where are you going, Connie?" The fog was so thick you couldn't see the bow of the boat. It was obvious I wasn't going anywhere. Even I had to laugh. After a time we made it through the narrows as we had in the fog at Seguin. What a relief when we sailed into the harbor and realized the men were the best of navigators. All in all it was a wonderful trip.

We'd also have picnic trips with the Bunkers, their relatives, and friends. A frequent visitor was Bob Brinkerhoff, a syndicated cartoonist. Once Doctor asked Bob whom he would choose as a companion if he were stranded on an island. To the amazement of the sixteen guests, the reply was, "Elson Small. He is the most versatile man I know."

Once Ruth Bunker and her sister Kathy capsized and needed rescuing by Elson during a summer gale. Elson had gone to Calais for supplies in the speedboat because the weather was sunny and calm and he wanted to save time. While he was gone one of those quick summer storms came up. I worried for fear the speedboat wouldn't be seaworthy enough for him to get back.

There were a lot of pleasure boats on the river at the time. One small sail yacht trying for Jones' Beach came into our cove to escape the worst of the storm. Elson had been just nearing the island when a heavy gust of wind hit. He went into the cove to tell the owner of the boat to stay there and not try to make the mainland mooring, then took off down the river to the spot where the Bunker girls with their small sailboat were floating.

I stood on the bank, watching the little speedboat now high on the waves, then out of sight. I was praying he would make it and make it he did. Kathy, about seventeen, had considered swimming to shore, but Ruth, about twelve, had a good knowledge of boats and navigation and thought it best they cling to the boat until help came. That help was Elson, who got them ashore.

Meanwhile, the owner of the boat in our cove decided that if the speedboat could weather the gale, he could make Jones' Beach. He started out of the cove, but only cleared the mouth before the sails were blown away. Somehow he got into shelter of land and anchored.

Our friendship with Ruth Bunker lasted over the years. She married in 1943 and in a few years, as Ruth Ellis, visited us in the winter for two weeks. We were so happy and excited at her letter saying she was coming for a visit, especially as she was bringing her eight-month-old son, Timothy. Edward, her husband, a lieutenant in the Marines, had been sent to the Pacific, and Ruth, who had been living in Encinitas while he was at the Marine base near there, planned to drive home to Calais to be with her parents until Eddie came back. Another Marine wife was coming with her, but at the last moment couldn't make it, so Ruth started out alone with baby Timothy. In Ohio she was driving on a long stretch of highway, feeling exhausted, when she saw a Marine on the side of the road, trying to thumb a ride. It wasn't dangerous then to pick up hitchhikers, but even so Ruth had reservations. However, she felt it was almost as though Eddie were saying, "He's my buddy, help him." Ruth stopped and found he was a boy she knew slightly from a town near Calais. Seeing how exhausted she was, he took over and drove all the way to Maine and home.

Elson went to Red Beach to pick up Ruth and Timothy. I wondered what we could do to entertain her, but she came prepared with a picture of the Ellis coat of arms she wanted me to draw on canvas, so she could work it in needlepoint as a surprise for Eddie. We had fun working the colors, and it came out just beautiful.

During their two-week stay we put chairs around the couch to make a temporary crib for Timothy. Looking up from our work, we were surprised to see Tim holding onto the chairs, dancing up and down. He became famous for taking his first step on historic Dochet's Island.

We had a heavy snowfall the night before Ruth had to leave. I can still see Elson with Timothy on his shoulders, followed by Ruth, wading to the boat house in snow up to their hips. I missed them so much after they left.

The Joneses were another family who were summer friends. One warm day a large rowboat we could recognize as an Asa Pede model, made in Red Beach, was halfway to the light before we noticed it. We heard voices and were introduced to the Jones girls. The family had arrived from Port Huron, Michigan, and was staying in the Jones homestead for the summer. When Mr. Jones had left Red Beach to settle in Port Huron, he kept his Red Beach residence for a summer home and the girls enjoyed it to the full. The girls were Alice, Evelyn, Betty, Mary, and Helen. Helen would bring a friend, Kaye Masterson, for the summer and these six girls were sources of fun and true friendship.

They often rowed out to the island bringing corn, vegetables, and hamburgers to roast on the beach and would invite us down to enjoy the food with them. They taught us to love an evening around the camp fire and gave us lessons in astronomy. I learned how to find the Big Dipper and the North Star, the Little Dipper and the Milky Way, and learned also how important the North Star was to navigation. We had many discussions on current events as well. Sometimes we all slept out on the beach in our sleeping bags.

One night they had been out to our house for dinner when a thick fog blew in. At about ten o'clock when they started for home, Elson gave them explicit instructions on how to keep the sound of the bell over the stern of the boat. We saw them disappear into the fog. Elson then proceeded to wind the bell which was about ready to stop. We heard someone hollering "Ship ahoy" in the fog and realized it was the Jones girls back. We all had a good laugh, for after Elson's concern and instructions, he had silenced the bell by winding it and they were lost. They were always teasing Elson, but this time was one on them. They told him they had made Wilson's buoy, across from the island, three times before landing back at the island.

Another time, Elson had taken the Jones girls and me to Saint Andrews in our powerboat. He had special business with the Canadian customs officials and told Evelyn and Kaye to buy him a mop for cleaning up the boat, while he conducted his business. I waited in the boat. When Elson and the officials emerged from the building, the Jones girls were waiting. Much to Elson's embarrassment, the girls marched in front of him. Evelyn, with the mop, acted as marshal. Betty, Kaye, and Helen pretended they were playing instruments as they all escorted Elson and the official out the long dock to the boat. He discreetly tried to motion them away, but they pretended they didn't notice. He was so angry when they got to the boat, he said he wasn't going to let the leaders ride in the power boat. He put the two of them in the dinghy and towed them home. However, instead of thinking this a punishment, they had much more fun and felt quite special.

Tourists and summer visitors to the Saint Croix River were drawn to the sandbank on Dochet's and to the light. They played on the sand and beach, sliding down the bank. One day a couple and their little girl and Elson and I were talking on the beach, when the child said she was thirsty. I invited her to walk up to the house with me to get a drink of water.

She skipped joyously over the pasture, chatting gaily until we came to the gate. Our cow stood in front of the gate, so I said, "Now, Nancy, you get out of our way, so we can get through the gate."

The little girl stopped short. Eyes flashing, she indignantly said, "Most little girls wouldn't like having a cow called Nancy." For a moment this outburst had me at a loss, then I realized her name must be Nancy.

"Well, you see, if I had a little girl, I'd call her Nancy. As we didn't have a little girl and we loved our cow, I called her Nancy."

I wish you could have seen her face light up. She asked, "Please, may I touch her?" Every year until Nancy was in college she came to see me and my Nancy.

Another visitor was not so pleasant. As at Seguin, there were a few who thought we were freaks because we lived at a light on an island. Sometimes titled visitors from England who stayed at the Algonquin Hotel in Saint Andrews came to the island with their families, governesses, and maids. One day I had guests for dinner and had my table all set nice, when I heard a rap at the front door. In my apron, I went to the door to find several English tourists who wanted to see the light. They had to go through the house to get to the light built like a cupola on top and acted as if I wasn't fit to answer their questions. One came down the stairs, put her hands on her hips as she looked around my house, and sighting the table, said, "Well, you have almost anything anybody else has. You even have a radio." One of my guests, a lawyer friend from the area, wanted to say something back to her, but I motioned her to be quiet. Luckily, only a few of our visitors were unpleasant.

I never tired of the beauty of the Saint Croix River and the island. If one of us went ashore it was usually Elson, and on days when I had to stay and tend the light I'd often walk around the island. One particular day I had made my rounds of coves, ledges, and sand beaches, stopping to dig a clam that had made its hiding place known by a spurt of water from a small hole in the sand left by the ebbing tide. A little sandpiper showed no fear of me, his legs a blur as he ran back and forth at the edge of the water searching for food.

I climbed the bank and sat watching the cars on the mainland filled with people hurrying to go places. Boats filled with vacationers sailed up and down the river. Laughing voices carrying across the calm water.

I was a little lonesome alone on an island in the middle of the Saint Croix River, wishing I could join the activity on shore. Elson visited and talked with people, joining in the daily discussions. He usually returned to the island, mind refreshed, having been a participator. I, on the other hand, was an observer, with little mental challenge but for the nature which surrounded me. So, I turned to nature and the animals, learning that nothing is sufficient unto itself.

One sunny day, warm with a brisk wind flowing from the southwest, I was alone on the island while Elson went for supplies. Walking in the cove, picking up stones and shells, I noticed a can bumping up and down, pounding against the rocks a little beyond the surf. The water formed a white lace over the rocks and swirled the kelp to and fro. I watched the can for a while, then, thinking the shape was interesting, waded out and picked it up.

Though the can was black, a small bright spot shone through. I knew it must be brass, so went up to the house to clean it with brass polish. I couldn't believe my eyes. As I rubbed on one side, the inscription "USLSS — Powder" shone through. Memories flooded back to me.

As a small child I had watched as ships' crews were rescued by my father and the other men of the Lifesaving Service. During a bad storm, flares were be fired from ships in trouble. The lifesaving crew would go up Creath's Hill right by our house with the cart filled with ropes wound around drums. The ropes were attached to cannon and shot over the top of the crippled ship so survivors could be brought in in the breeches buoy or bosun's chair, which looked like a ring with pants attached. A powder can with extra powder for the cannon was always carried and I often "helped" my father carry this very can, curling my finger around the bail, thinking I was doing a big job!

After days of cleaning, I got the verdigris off the brass enough to show the beauty of the metal. My feeling was that this was a special gift to me, carried sixty or more miles through narrows and islands over the years for me to find it; a mystery I still don't understand.

If a crew had to be brought to the island to do major repairs, feeding them was a lot easier here than on Avery Rock or Seguin. At low tide we dug all the clams we needed in the flats around the island. Elson fished enough lobster traps to keep us in lobsters and we went line fishing for haddock and flounder. We had a cow for milk, cream, and butter; a garden; and our own hens. Wild duck was plentiful in season and goose tongue greens abundant. Coffee, tea, sugar, flour, and fresh meat were about all we had to buy ashore.

After we decided to have a garden, the problem was how to plow the ground. When Elson decided he'd buy an old truck of some kind and bring it to the island, we went ashore to see what he could find. Finally, at Keene Lake, he found an old Model T Ford that had been stripped of its body, leaving only the chassis, gas tank, instrument panel, engine, and steering wheel. The engine ran, so he bought it.

On the way home Elson bought some logs and planks and towed them over to Dochet's, where the next day he started building a raft strong enough to hold the truck. Gerald came down from Calais for the weekend and he and Elson went to Keene Lake to pick up the truck. Since the vehicle wasn't licensed or in condition to be driven on the highway, they devised a hitch that enabled them to tow it behind the car, Gerald sitting on top of the empty gas tank holding onto the steering wheel, trying to steer as best he could. But the trip became quite difficult, for Elson couldn't slow down enough to allow easy steering and they soon discovered the brakes didn't work. Gerald hollered to Elson to slow down so he could keep the truck from zigzagging all over the road, but Elson would holler back, "I can't slow down or you'll run into me." So, for about two miles they attracted a lot of attention, but they made it to Plaster Mill Point where the raft had been beached, without collision or damage to anyone or anything.

By this time enough men had gathered for them to have plenty of help getting the truck onto the raft, which had been beached at three-quarter tide ebb to allow them time enough to bring the truck from Keene Lake and secure it before the raft floated again. The raft and truck were towed over to the island without any trouble.

The raft couldn't be beached in the cove as the bank was too high to drive the truck up over it, so they beached on the west side of the island which sloped gradually to the rocks with just a little bank. I held my breath as they drove the truck up over the bank, for fear it would stall partway up and roll back, but it went up like it wanted to be a part of our island life.

I had to learn how to drive the truck and found it wasn't easy to get the spark throttle on the steering wheel just right so when I worked the clutch with my foot the engine wouldn't stall. Elson had also bought a plow from the man who sold him the truck. He hitched the plow to the back of the truck and I'd drive back and forth, making furrows. I tried so hard to make them straight, but Doctor Bunker said they were the crookedest straight furrows he had ever seen. It was hard to regulate the speed and sometimes I'd go too fast for Elson to keep up at the plow. I don't think we ever did get the right pace.

Besides the gardens, the cow also was important to our food supply. But sometimes I had misgivings about owning one. One August day we had invited Doctor and Mrs. Bunker, Doctor and Mrs. Weeks, and Mr. and Mrs. Brinkerhoff over for a picnic. We spread our cloth on the boat house platform instead of going to the beach because it was so pretty looking upriver to the cross of the Saint Croix which had inspired Sieur de Monts to name it the Saint Croix.

I knew Mr. Brinkerhoff had expressed a desire for a blueberry pie so I had made one for dessert. We finished our main course of lobster, clams, green peas, and corn, and I started for the pie. To my surprise and dismay, Blossom, our cow at the time, stood with her nose deep in my pie. She raised her head at my approach, her nose all blue, juice running from her mouth as her big brown eyes said, "It's very delicious."

Mr. Brinkerhoff jumped up and sketched the picture, which he used in his syndicated cartoon "Little Mary Mix-Up." When I apologized to him for not having a pie for him, he replied, "I would have loved that pie, but this was worth much more," so we all laughed and petted Blossom and hoped she would not have a stomachache. That was a great change of heart for me because ever since I was a child I had been terrified of cows. I would have terrible nightmares of them coming to trample me. After Elson brought Blossom to the island, I would crawl down a steep bank and walk around the shore to the beach so I wouldn't have to go through the pasture where the cow was grazing.

One night Elson was to be taken into the Masons. As he went into the tower to light the lamp before going ashore, he hollered to me to bring Blossom into the barn and tie her up. I wanted to help him get started ashore and also did not want him to know I was afraid. As I went over to the cow, my whole insides turned over in fright. At first I thought I could take the end of the rope farthest away from her and pull her at a distance into the barn. But this didn't work, for Blossom thought I was taking her to a fresher ground to feed and came lumbering over to my side. I could feel her body and smell the fresh, grass odor of her breath. I just had to muster up the courage to get near enough to reach the halter. Not knowing what I was going through, Blossom started off beside me, as quickly and as quietly as she could, right into the barn, where my shaking hands tied her to the stanchion.

Just then Elson came out of the house, looked at me,

and quickly said, "What is the matter? Did the cow hurt you?" He was so concerned, I must have shown all my suffering in my face. I told him about my fear of cows and why I was so terrified those nights when he had to wake me from my nightmares.

"Why, Blossom is as harmless as our cat," he said. Then, "I have just time to make it ashore to meet the men who are taking me to the Lodge at Calais." He showed me how to milk and left.

Well, that was some experience! The cow was safely tied and looking for her portion of grain, which I gave her. Then I started to milk. I had thought it would be easy, but when I tried, I got not a drop of milk. I experimented and finally a small stream came. I would never get a pailful the way it was going. Even my cat was disgusted when I couldn't squirt a stream of warm milk into her mouth like Elson did. I found that if I used both hands to squeeze I had more success. By then Blossom knew something was very wrong with this new farmer and turned to look at me. Afraid she would get uneasy, I gave her more grain to distract her. Soon an hour and a half had passed and Blossom had had an overdose of grain. I was unable to do the stripping which I had been told gave the cream of the milk, so when Elson came home he finished milking. He also informed me I had been feeding the cow chicken feed instead of cow feed. I slept fitfully all night for fear I had hurt the cow, but she seemed none the worse for the experience. Incidentally, it broke my fear of cows.

The milking wasn't the end of the evening. When I'd gotten cleaned up and the barn odors erased from my hands, I decided to iron the clothes I had washed that day. I was alone on the island except for Blossom; my tiger cat; and Peter, the canary, who was safely covered in his cage. I was finishing my last piece of laundry when I heard what I thought was a woman calling in distress. I was so concerned, I worked up a case of anxiety wondering who was out there on the river and what I would do if someone came into the house. Just then the kitchen door opened. No one appeared. I was prepared to throw my hot iron at any intruder, for I really thought someone was killing that woman.

At ten o'clock at night I was all alone on the island just praying Elson would come. A few minutes later he did come and eventually convinced me that what I'd heard was a loon calling. Ten o'clock at night alone on an island in the middle of a river is not a good time or place to hear your first loon. Elson also quieted my fears by deciding that a light breeze hand sprung up and blown open the unlatched kitchen door. I sure was glad to have him home; I almost forgot to congratulate him on his acceptance into Masonry.

Our cow was featured in one of a series of publicity photos for the Coast Guard intended to encourage men to enlist in the service. Just after the war a Coast Guard commander came to Dochet's and took the picture of Elson milking the cow. It was released for publication with the following information: "One of the strange sights a Coast Guardsman takes in his stride is this of a Chief Boatswain's Mate milking a cow. This is not a rolling pasture of a mid-western farm, however, but a tiny island off the Atlantic coast. Lighthouse Keeper Elson Small tends the chores around St. Croix River Light, Red Beach, Maine." The photo was printed in newspapers and magazines all over the country and many clippings were sent to me. It was interesting that under the pictures published in various papers, no two captions were alike.

We had several cats in our years on Dochet's, the most famous of which was Scottie. We had waited ten years before we felt we could buy a car. No one could have been more excited or proud than we were the day we went up to Calais and came home with the brand-new Pontiac. To celebrate, we took time off and went to Lubec to visit my sister Alice. She had two darling kittens just old enough to play, one a tiger, the other, two yellow eyes peeking out of a ball of black, fluffy fur.

It was hard to choose when Alice asked if I wouldn't like to take one home, but the little black one seemed to take to me and I fell in love with him. Because he looked like a little Scottie dog, I named him Scottie. I felt guilty taking him away from his playmate, though he didn't seem to mind the forty-mile trip back to Dochet's at all. First he played in the front seat, then in the back, finally settling in my lap for a nap. Scottie began to grow to his big paws and big eyes and broad nose. His fur was long, his ears like velvet. He was fifteen pounds of muscle and a big armful to pick up.

In our dining room, I had a wicker plant stand about three feet long, with a shelf underneath on which we made a comfortable bed for Scottie. He was trained not to get up on my nice furniture or jump on my beds. Sometimes, when he was very naughty, Elson shook the fly swatter at him and he would obediently go to his bed, where he lay switching his tail back and forth, his big yellowy eyes saying, "All right, I mind today, but you just wait. "

One cold, moonlit night we missed Scottie. Looking for him, I opened the stair door. He rushed by me and went straight to the outside door. I knew what he had done. He loved to get upstairs and jump in my feather ticks. The three beds with feather ticks on them were a disaster after he'd had his fun. I let him out, but he was gone such a long time I was getting worried about him since it was very cold. Finally I heard him scratching on the door to come in. Imagine my surprise when he rushed by me dragging a wild duck by the neck! Taking it into the kitchen, he dropped it in the middle of the floor, and immediately went to his bed, as much as to say, "There, I have paid you for messing up your beds." The duck wasn't even hurt, so Elson put it in the barn, and later, when fresh food was scarce, we had it for dinner.

Scottie loved clams. All around the island were flats full of delicious, large clams we could dig with a stick. I'd start the hole, but Scottie couldn't wait and would put his big paws in the hole and try to get the clam out.

We both loved to hold Scottie, and he was a lapful! Above the plant stand was my canary in his cage; Scottie never once tried to harm him. I think he felt he had to take care of him as part of the family.

One Friday night I was picking over the beans, getting them ready to put on to soak, when one dropped on the floor, rolling under the stove. Scottie chased it, brought it back, and laid it at my feet. I picked it up and tossed it again, and he did the same thing. I made a little yarn ball for him to play this game of toss and bring.

Later, we left Dochet's for a time during World War II and had to let Scottie go to some dear friends in Aroostook County who wanted him. They took Scottie in June and we went up to visit on a vacation in October. To the amazement of everybody, the first thing Scottie did when he saw me was to go get the little yarn ball and we played the toss and throw game again. No one else had been able to get him to do this. He had a wonderful life at the farm, visiting other farms miles apart and always returning to his new home. A newspaper article made him quite a famous cat, so famous that people came specially to see him.

Getting ashore was relatively easy from Dochet's. Although sometimes the river was rough and often there was fog, we did not need the forty-five-foot Jonesport boat. After Elson sold that, he heard of a boat he thought would be just right. When my father had been at the Quoddy Head Lifesaving Station he had often helped man the twenty-foot surfboat. When the old service was taken over by the Coast Guard, a new station was built farther down on Quoddy Head and the surfboat sold to Jerome Creath who made it over into a motorboat. Elson heard Jerome wanted to sell it and we bought it. Gerald and Grace came down from Calais in November 1931, and on a beautiful, summerlike day, drove us to Lubec. Elson and Gerald sailed the boat from Lubec to Dochet's, while Grace and I drove back to Red Beach and rowed over to the island to be there when the men returned, sunburned and tired. Elson and I discarded many names before we finally decided to take a part of our two names and call her the *Elcon*. She served us well all our stay at Dochet's, this boat which had also served my father so well.

We almost lost the *Elcon* once. Old Man Winter had descended in all his fury. When Elson finally decided to go ashore to get the mail, the wind was strong and the water was rough at the slip, so he pushed the rowboat off, rowing down into the cove, in the lea, before starting the outboard motor. On the way out, he noticed that the *Elcon* and the tender had disappeared from their winter quarters. He saw the *Elcon* on some rocks high up on the bank above where she had been hauled out. He later found the tender full of ice and sticks, frozen in the sand; the cradle the *Elcon* had been resting on was also in the sand of the cove.

When we went down to the boats after Elson returned from the mainland, we couldn't believe what we saw. It was as though a mighty hand had lifted the boat from its cradle and placed it high up on the bank between two rocks. The tides were not running high, so the only answer we could think of was that there had been a tidal wave sometime in the night. Later we read of the unusually high tide that had done thousands of dollars of damage in Lubec. We were thankful to the good Lord, for had the wind been in another direction, both boats would have been total losses.

Although getting ashore from Dochet's was easy compared to the other lights we'd been on, there were still problems. Soon after we went to Dochet's we were invited ashore for dinner with Evadve and Arthur Cook and their mother. We had a delicious dinner and a very interesting afternoon, especially since Elson discovered that Arthur had been his replacement as second mate ten years before, when he left the sea for the lights. The day drew close to sundown. We weren't used to the tides and when we reached the point where our boat was tied, we were amazed to find her high and dry, with an expanse of flats seemingly halfway to the light.

We were all dressed up and it looked as though we were not going to get back to the island in time to light the light. Elson said the only thing we could do was to take off our shoes, roll up our clothes, and wade out in the muck. He rolled his pants to his knees, tied the laces of his shoes together, and put them around his necking, telling me to do the same. Mine didn't have laces so I had to carry them; I pulled up my dress as far as was decent. We stepped into the muck up to our knees and finally reached the dinghy. One on each side, we took hold of the gunnels and lifted and slid her along in the slimy mud until we reached the channel where she floated. In the boat we realized our feet and legs were all cut and bleeding from the clamshells we'd trudged over. So faithful were keepers then, they would face any danger to have their light lit on time. We succeeded that day.

We had been on Dochet's eight months when I joined the church at Red Beach by having my letter transferred from Bucks Harbor. Each Wednesday, weather permitting, I went ashore to work with the Circle members. On one of these Wednesday Circle meeting days, Elson was very busy with his station work so I took the rowboat and rowed ashore, feeling a bit nervous about whether I could moor the boat right. But I had no trouble and went to the quilting bee they were having that day. We had such an interesting, happy time, I forgot my boat. When I got back it was high and dry.

I tried to drag it through the mud as we had before, but couldn't do it alone. Just then I heard a voice saying, "Wait, I'll help you." It was Henry Davis, a young boy I'd had in Sunday school and who lived in Red Beach. With his help I got the dinghy in the channel. I made it to the light before it got dark because of his welcome act of kindness.

Wearing good clothing when we went ashore was always risky. One winter Sunday, Elson and I were going to church. I was dressed in a handsome, new, gray suit; hat; and gloves. On the slip my feet went out from under me and I wallowed in the seaweed until Elson could get me out. We did not get to church that day.

On another winter day we were on our way to Eastport, where Elson had an appointment. At the Red

Beach landing, I, in my beaver-collar coat, slipped and ended up under the boat, up to my neck in water. Elson had to get to Eastport, so I wrung as much water as I could out of my clothes, we turned the car heater high, and I remained in the car, heater on, the whole time.

The problem of clothing was difficult, especially since we didn't dress casually in those days. I never wore a pair of pants until I was involved in some Red Cross work during the war. On Dochet's we finally resolved the problem by hiring a garage for the car in Red Beach and putting a wardrobe there. In it I placed all the clothes I would want to wear on shore. It was cold changing clothes in the garage in the winter, but better than ending up with muddy, wet clothing.

World War II brought great change into our lives. June 4, 1943, dawned in its perfect Saint Croix manner. We did our usual morning tasks around the light and early in the afternoon looked over our freshly planted vegetable garden. The river was glassy, the afternoon, hot. We decided to rest before going into Calais for supplies. Then, at about four o'clock, we heard an auto horn and saw the signal flag go up on the signal pole at the Red Beach boat landing. It was Bosun Mate First Charles Whitney from Quoddy Head Coast Guard Station. Elson went after him. As they landed, I saw that Mr. Whitney brought a seabag and a box of groceries, and I knew that our stay on Dochet's was being interrupted.

Charles Whitney had transfer orders. In three hours Elson was to report to the base at Eastport to take charge of a patrol boat. I had a couple of hours to pack his seabag and my bag, get supper, and try to think to pack things that were so personal we didn't want strangers to see them. For me this was a disturbing time. I was so very upset to think I had to walk out of my home and leave our possessions to a stranger who would take over the light.

When we first went into the Lighthouse Service it was under civil service, so our dwellings were furnished with our own belongings, not helped by the government. The Coast Guard took over the Lighthouse Service in 1939, turning it into a military service. We hadn't been warned at all of this transfer of Elson's, and I'll admit I was at a loss. One thing I knew was that I couldn't stay there on Dochet's with a strange man, so I stepped out into a dark world, knowing only that I would be with my husband a few hours longer; I didn't dare to think beyond that.

It was wartime. Everyone was upset in some way, so I tried to make the best of our situation. Fortunately, Mr. Whitney could milk a cow, since we had not time to sell ours or make provision for her elsewhere. We left Dochet's, not knowing when we would return or when we would move our belongings.

After we arrived in Eastport just in time for Elson to report to the base, I found myself alone in the dark in a strange city. I went to the hotel as Elson had recommended and took the last available room. I was alone, one of the very few times Elson and I had been apart since we were married.

The next morning I went looking for a place to stay. Someone told me about a boardinghouse on Key Street run by a Mrs. Pottle, so I went down and rented one of her rooms. At first I didn't have much to do when Elson was out three or four days at a time on the patrol boat besides go across to Lubec on the ferry to spend time with my mother. This, however, got too expensive. Mrs. Pottle introduced me to another boarder, Helen Disney, sister of Walt Disney. Miss Disney was connected with the U.S.O. and the Red Cross and spent time in Eastport and other cities. She got me interested in Red Cross work and took me with her when she visited the families of servicemen. One evening we talked in her black coupe at the side of the road for over an hour waiting for a blinding rainstorm to stop. She fascinated me with talk of her experiences and volunteer work.

When I was busy I felt all right, even though away from my home, and often Elson. Sometimes I ate alone at the hotel and would write my thoughts. Some I have saved:

HOTEL, EASTPORT, MAINE, JUNE 25, 1943

"Private thoughts written while lonesome, waiting for my dinner at the hotel. I have wasted three nice envelopes.

"May God go with Elson and make this day and tomorrow a success. He is worth more than pleasure, so if life becomes dull I hope God's goodness will become a part of me inasmuch as I can be a good wife and companion to him.

"There are times we wonder what is best, but if we can't do our best at all times it may be an indication we are not developing as fast or as successfully as we should.

"Keep the mind busy, for it will help to settle our restless spirits. Can we adjust ourselves when we go back to the same routine after such a busy, broken month?

"The supper hour here at the hotel is 6 P.M. It's cool here now and I hope it stays cool so we can sleep. This has been the first hot day. Elson couldn't be with me, so I am eating alone here at the hotel.

Mrs. Potter is better after a severe heart attack. All the Coast Guard boys are eating supper here. Hope they have something nice for them to eat.

"Will go up to see Caroline if I can and hope it doesn't squall. Day and night we do things that keep our thoughts pure.

" 'There are times we wonder what is best and if we can't do our best at all times it may be an indication we are not developing as fast or as successfully as we should.' This thought seems to go through my mind often.

"The lady at the next table is writing too, and I wonder if she is lonesome and talking to her inner self.

"Dinner at last and very delicious. I'll take my time to eat it, for if I eat slowly it will consume more time from my room.

"Somehow, though, I find friends and am too busy to just think. This military atmosphere gives me courage, for if Elson is doing his part patrolling the submarine-infested waters, I can do mine by being the kind of person he would want to come back to."

After Miss Disney left Mrs. Pottle's, I was lonely at the boardinghouse, so after spending a rainy day alone in my room, I decided to seek another place to live.

I went to Beckett's Candy Store downstreet. When I was about twelve my mother had a grocery and candy store and bought her sweets from Mr. Beckett. When the order came there was always a special little box for me. Now Mr. Beckett was retired from his wholesale and retail candy and bakery business, but he kept the candy store, as he said, "to keep me from the rocking chair."

I hadn't seen Mr. Beckett in twenty-five years, but

when I asked if he remembered me, he answered, "I surely do, and your lovely mother."

I told him my problem. He said, "Well, Mrs. B. would never take strangers into her home, but you go up and tell her I sent you."

Nervously I rang the doorbell. When I told Mrs. Beckett who I was and that her husband had sent me, she asked me into a lovely room where we visited. She also remembered my mother and as we talked we found I went to her church, we both liked to make things, and we had other interests in common. When I excused myself to go, she said, "I'd like to show you my daisy room upstairs." We went up the stairs to a large room with four large windows draped with ruffled organdy curtains embroidered with daisies. The beautiful brass bed was covered with a yellow daisy bedspread. Two bureaus, a couple of chairs, and a green plush carpet completed the furnishings.

After I'd admired the room we went downstairs and I had started to open the street door when she said, "I suppose you'll be moving in by Thursday?"

I guess I surprised her when I replied, "You mean, I can come stay in that beautiful, sunshine room?" From that moment we became friends. The Becketts remained dear friends until their deaths, long after I had moved to other places.

Eastport was a small city, and seemingly overnight, thousands of Seabees and their families descended on the town. Everything was filled to capacity that fall; many walked the streets, cold and troubled, looking for places to live. I'll always remember Eastport as a great city because wealthy and poor alike opened their homes to give families shelter until they could get accommodations.

During this time meat was scarce. When a little came into the city, people stood in long lines hoping to get some. Mr. Beckett, being a pillar of the community, knew beforehand when meat was available, but refused to take advantage of his position to avoid his rightful turn. As Mrs. Beckett was unable to stand in the long, slow lines, I would go for their meat rations and for mine. I usually went home with a less tender piece or a soupbone, but that was fine with them. Once I went to get three pork chops. A man in line saw them and knew there were no more. With tears in his eyes, he said, "I have a family of four children and we've had no meat for a long time." He turned to go. The meatman handed me the chops. I turned and gave them to the man, telling him they were from Mr. Beckett. When I told Mr. Beckett, he approved what I had done.

At Thanksgiving and Christmas I helped Mr. Beckett make candy at his store. He could tell by the smell when peanut brittle was just right. At Christmas I helped him make ribbon candy and candy canes and angel hair, like spun glass. He was rationed to a certain amount of sugar and knew that he couldn't supply all who wanted the candy, so he ordered that candy be sold first to families with children, then to others if it lasted. I admired the Becketts for these values and felt lucky they were my friends.

Elson was sent to radio school in Boston and was at the base in Boston several times after finishing the school. The Touraine Hotel seemed to be the headquarters for service personnel and families, so that is where I stayed. I spent my days roaming around in stores. Elson said he always knew where to find me, for I always headed for the arts-and-crafts section. Nights he would be with me at the hotel. After his duty was over at the base, he went back to Eastport and his patrol boat, the C.G.R. 79.

While he was in radio school, Elson was sent to New York, and I went with him to visit a friend for five or six days. Returning to Boston in the early evening we went to the Touraine to get a room. But when Elson asked the desk clerk about the room he was informed there were none available at that moment, but if we would wait a while some provisions could surely be made. Elson knew the manager, who soon was motioning us to follow him. We were surprised when he opened a door to a lovely suite of rooms. We had had a vision of having to sit out the night in the lobby of the hotel and here we were sitting in easy chairs in a sitting room. The manager said, "Don't look so astonished and bewildered. Even in wartime there are good people and Admiral Starkey [not his real name] is one of them."

The admiral had been standing near the desk when the discussion about the room was going on and told the manager to put us in his rooms as his wife was in Hawaii and would not be back for two days, and he was going out on an emergency for two weeks. The manager told us "Just relax and enjoy it. There will be a room available for you tomorrow."

At two o'clock in the morning the telephone rang. It was on my side of the bed, so I answered it. When I said hello, there was a slight pause, then a lady asked in a very cool voice, "Is this Admiral Starkey's suite?" I said yes, and the voice exploded.

"What are you doing in my husband's suite at 2 A.M.? Put him on the phone at once!"

"I'm sorry, Mrs. Starkey, but your husband is not here. He was shipped out six hours ago."

"Stop your stalling and put him on the phone!"

By this time Elson was awake, so I said, "Elson, she doesn't believe me. You talk to her."

She didn't believe Elson either. Finally he told her, "You call the manager and he will enlighten you."

About half an hour later the phone rang again, but I surely was not going to answer it. I gave the phone to Elson. It was Mrs. Starkey, wishing to apologize to us. She hadn't received the message left for her when she landed in California and hadn't known that her husband had been sent to sea. We thanked her and asked her to thank her husband for his kindness. I sure was glad Elson was there with me and not at the base!

Not long after this, Elson had orders to report to the base in Boston and from there to New York. He had decommissioned the C.G.R. 79, taking her to Gloucester, Massachusetts. When he came to my room at Mrs. Beckett's to tell me, he was very upset as it would be another change for me. We had just finished moving our furniture from Dochet's to Eastport, putting it in storage. From what he could tell me about his orders, this looked like an overseas assignment. I knew I could stay with Mrs. Beckett until we knew what was in store for us, so I tried to keep him cheered up and not worried about how I would make out.

A few days before Elson was to report to Boston, the Coast Guard officer above Elson came to Eastport. He was very perturbed that Elson was being sent to the pool. Elson had served in World War I, had a good record in this war, and was forty-five years old. Suddenly, while I was ironing his uniforms, Elson burst into the room, all excited. I couldn't believe what I heard. "We're going back to Dochet Island. Start packing!"

We spent Christmas with the Bunkers. They and the Becketts loaded us with goodies to take back to Dochet's.

When our loaded car reached Red Beach, Mr. Whitney was there to meet us with the rowboat. He and his wife helped us put our belongings on the boat, then left for Cutler Light Station where they had been transferred. Since the weather stayed good we went to Eastport every day to get what belongings we could fit in or on the car; we even managed chairs and a bed tied to the top, and bedding, linens, and dishes enough to camp with inside. The Coast Guard crew brought the rest of our furnishings a week later.

As suddenly as it had been interrupted, our life on Dochet Island began again. It went on as before, the summers active and full of friends; the winters, time to do the repairs and handiwork and boatbuilding.

Then, after twenty-six years spent on islands, Elson decided he'd like to be on the mainland. When he learned that Portsmouth Harbor Light, also called Fort Point Light, in New Castle, New Hampshire, was to be vacant, Elson asked to be transferred there. It was hard leaving a place where we had such pleasant memories. The inspectors told us we were leaving a little paradise and we knew it too. But, in April 1946, we packed our personal belongings and reported to West Quoddy Head Coast Guard Station and from there drove to our new home at New Castle.

P O R T S M O U T H   H A R B O R   L I G H T

We were not going to a light on the mainland after all.
On our way to our new home we stopped at a restaurant
in Portsmouth where Elson met a man who'd been on
the patrol boat with him. Answering the other's question as to why we left such a beautiful spot as Dochet
Island, Elson said he'd thought we'd like being on the
mainland after twenty-six years on islands. The man
laughed and said, "Well, I think you'll be surprised to
know that New Castle is also on an island." So, we
started on an island and we were to end on one.

However, this island was nothing like the ones we
were used to. It was really part of the mainland as it was
connected to it by a bridge and causeway. No longer did
we have to get in a boat to get the smallest item at a
store. At the other lights we had had to go by boat every
time we moved to do anything. Here it was heavenly
not to have to do a day's work before we even got to
where we were going. Now we could just get in a car or
walk.

Portsmouth Harbor Light was known locally by several names: Fort Point Light, New Castle Light, Fort Constitution Light. The lighthouse tower was located just outside the walls of Fort Constitution, on a point jutting out into Portsmouth Harbor. The fort was occupied by the army in 1946 and when we drove up to it, Peter the canary in his cage on my lap, we stopped at the gate to show our identification and were given a pass through.

Our dwelling was within the fort, surrounded by massive granite walls; openings in the walls showed where canons had been placed during the American Revolution. There were barracks, an old brick wall that had stood when Paul Revere took his historic ride through the fort, and dungeons. One day I went into one of the dungeons to see if I could capture the feeling of being imprisoned in such a place. I came out of that damp, dark, bare hole believing it was no place to put a human being for any reason. I was later told there were more dungeons under the granite pavements around the house. I surely hoped not.

I learned a little of the history of Portsmouth Harbor Light when I bought a charm of the lighthouse at Foye's Gift Center in Portsmouth. The commentary pointed out that the light had been in operation since before the Revolution and that the original had guided John Paul Jones and the *Ranger* into port in 1795. At about this same time, keeper Moses McFarland complained to the government about the high cost of living, so his salary was increased from $3.56 a week to $3.83 a week.

The present lighthouse was built in 1877. Long after we left Portsmouth Harbor Light, I worked at Mr. Foye's store and he would have me tell customers who bought the charm that I had lived in the lighthouse and that Elson and I were the last family to occupy it.

Our first few days at Portsmouth were very busy. Every keeper has his own way of running his station and usually changes are made. We washed a perfectly clean house, but I guess that's one of the duties that made it ours. Elson replaced Mr. Arnold White who, with his wife, was making his retirement home in New Castle. Both were very helpful to us.

On our second day, Elson and I took a walk around the fort area and the waterfront of the town of New Castle. The sun was out, the water a deep blue. An oil tanker, a passenger ship, any small craft sailed in and out of the harbor. On our return to the dwelling we passed one of the vacant barracks, where a cat lay on the steps. White with various colored spots, she was so thin her sides seemed they might play a tune as they hit each other. To a cat lover it was a terrible sight. Like a scared, wild thing, she scampered away when I went toward her.

Two days later, I was out by the piles of deactivated bombs, which were stacked higher than my head around the fort area, when the cat peeked out from under a pile. I went to the house to get some milk and bread, but the cat had gone when I returned, so I left the dish of food out. Later on I found it empty so each day I took food out. It always disappeared, but several days passed before the cat would come to the dish while I was still there, and then only if I kept my distance.

We kept feeding the cat, calling her Spotty. A few weeks after we'd started, I left for Calais and Red Beach. Elson assured me he wouldn't forget to feed the cat and then wrote to me in Calais to say that the cat must have liked the food for she had brought four more cats to help her eat it.

Spotty continued to come to the back door to eat, alone for a few days, but then with a black cat as scrawny and wild as she which I decided must be one of her kittens. After about a month Spotty died and Blackie, as we had named the other, disappeared. We thought she was gone for good, but one day, as we worked in the tomato and cucumber garden we'd planted next to the garage by the fort wall, Blackie came over the top of the wall with a tiny, black kitten in her mouth. She came directly to Elson and me, laid the kitten at our feet, then scampered back over the wall. She made four more trips, each with a kitten in her mouth, but instead of bringing the rest to us she hid them under the bombs.

We took our kitten in the house and petted it and gave it milk. A short time later, I heard Blackie crying at the door. She had come for her kitten. When I put it down on the step, Blackie took it under the bombs with the others. The next morning when I went over to the area where Blackie had taken the kittens, five pair of yellow eyes peered at me from the spaces between the bombs. I called, "kitty, kitty," and the little ball of black fur ran to me, so I picked it up and cuddled it as Blackie watched me closely. I did this daily until finally Blackie would allow the other kittens to come to the dish when I was there. We named our black kitten, Blackie II.

When winter set in, Elson built a little house for the cat and kittens on the front porch, which had a three-foot-high wall around it that protected the animals from storms. Blackie II spent a lot of time with us, but every night her mother would come crying for her. Though she got very tame, it was evident that she was torn between the man and woman in the house and her mother and brothers and sisters in their house on the porch. At the same time, the arrangement seemed to be fun for her.

At four o'clock one morning I was awakened by Blackie making the strangest cries. A sleet storm in the night had coated everything with ice. I hurried to see what was wrong. Blackie was like something wild and the nearest to letting me touch her she had ever been, as she ran away, then stopped to see if I was coming, all with that pitiful cry as she led me from place to place. The kittens were not in their house, so I decided that they must have been trapped someplace where Blackie couldn't get to them. Nowhere could I find any of them. I knew something dreadful must have happened.

Returning to the house, I told Elson. He was as puzzled as I. For two weeks we hunted everywhere, but never found my tame kitten or the other four. A sad, unresolved mystery. Someone at the store told me there were several dogs running wild; perhaps they had run the kittens into the river or the harbor.

The day we left New Castle for good a couple of years later, I was feeling badly that we couldn't take Blackie with us, but she wouldn't allow us to catch her and would have to be abandoned again. I was sitting on the granite steps when she suddenly came around the corner of the house and jumped right into my lap, making me pleased and happy that at last she was tamed. In my happiness I lifted my hand to pat her, but she scampered away. That was the last I saw of Blackie.

We had come to Portsmouth in April, expecting that our furniture would follow us any day. We'd sold our oak dining set so we went shopping for another, finding a solid mahogany one at a warehouse half-price sale. It was a beauty and looked so nice in our new home, but it was about the only furniture we had for all of May. Not until June first did we receive notice that a van would pick up our furniture in Red Beach to move it to

Portsmouth. Elson couldn't get away, so I had to take the train to Calais, then find a crew of men and a boat to move everything off Dochet's. Fortunately two friends in Red Beach came to my rescue, took charge of the operation, and rowed me to the island.

I was sick when I saw where my furniture and bedding was. The new keeper had naturally gotten tired of the long delay, and wanting the room we had stored the furniture in, moved it all out into the barn. Mattresses were ruined as a result of being folded with heavy furniture piled on them. My ninety-eight-piece set of Noritake china was packed away and I dreaded opening the box, afraid there would be a lot of breakage, but it was all intact.

We used Elson's raft to transport the furniture to shore. My piano had not been moved to the barn so it was in good shape; however, as the crew took it out on the raft I held my breath for fear it would tip over into the river or get wet. But they did a good job and it got safely to shore.

With our furnishings installed, our house at Portsmouth Harbor was nice. The large, fourteen-by-twenty kitchen was painted a beautiful shade of aqua-green. One of my favorite memories is of a silver pitcher, won by Elson in a powerboat race, filled with Betty Prior roses and set against the aqua wall.

What a wonderful feeling it was to have a phone, refrigerator, and electricity! Even the light was electric. We went on a buying spree and purchased a washing machine, coffee percolator, iron, toaster, and refrigerator. It was heaven.

Portsmouth Harbor was quite a change; to see such large ships as ocean liners, oil tankers, and Navy ships coming close to the light was not something we were used to. The harbor was very busy with large and small boats. One day Elson and I were in the rowboat, rowing because the outboard motor wouldn't start. A large Socony oil tanker bore down on us. I tried to row hard enough to get out of her path, but she was coming right toward us. As Elson tried to get the engine going, I put my back into it and rowed as hard as I could, thinking if that thing doesn't get us, the waves it makes will. People on board saw us but could do nothing. A ship that big would take miles to change direction. So, Elson kept puttering and I kept rowing, hard enough so we just squeezed out of the way of the prow. Then I stopped rowing and held on to the boat for dear life riding the waves. As the ship got abreast of us, the mate hollered, "If you would use Socony, you wouldn't have that trouble." Elson shouted back, "That is what I'm using."

I loved to sit by the tower watching the oil tankers and other boats go by, the smaller ones with their outboard motors skipping in and out around the larger. One day I took my usual stroll on the beach after watching the boats. The night before, the beach had been filled with people fishing for silverfish. This seemed to be an annual event, with people wading in to catch with their hands the fish which came in close to shore, shining like silver in the moonlight. The tide hadn't risen high enough to wash away the footprints and at the side of one I saw something shine in the sun. I stooped over, brushed the sand away from the object, and discovered the spout to a brass can I recognized as the kind we had used to carry alcohol to the tower to heat the kerosene mantles of some types of lamps we'd tended. I began searching for more pieces of the can and found the handle by the water, partly covered with sand. Now I was excited at my find and knew the rest of the can must be buried somewhere. I dug up the main part by the tower. On the side were the words, "USLH Depot Three District Lampshop Staten Island, N.Y." I took the pieces to Portsmouth and had them soldered together.

The can had been surveyed, or thrown overboard, as no good. I worked hard on it, polishing the brass to get back its beauty. It has a few dents and the traces of solder, but I have a treasure that I now use as a watering can for my plants, telling them they have to produce a lot of blossoms since they are watered with a famous can.

Part of my duties at Portsmouth Light was to fly the weather signals. These flags were flown to warn boats of gales, hurricanes, and just general weather conditions. The pennant, flown for small craft warnings, was red bunting in a triangular shape, eight by fifteen feet. There were also square flags, red with a black square in the center, measuring eight by eight feet, which when combined with the pennant, were for storm and hurricane warnings. The flags seldom lasted through a gale or hurricane without becoming so frayed new ones were needed. Some sections would still be good, and since I couldn't see throwing them away, I combined the colors with white fabric and made quilts out of them. I flew the flags unless they were soaking wet; then Elson would handle the very heavy fabric. At night, lanterns were hoisted for storm and hurricane warnings.

Instruments to measure atmospheric pressure and rainfall were located in back of the house. Every morning the captains of the tugboats and sometimes personnel from the navy yard called to find out what the visibility was from the light. Gathering this information was my job, as Elson had so many other duties to tend to.

Near the pressure and rain instruments in the back-yard grew a lovely Japanese quince tree. Under the tree I buried my canary, Peter. He'd been like a member of our family for eleven years before I brought him to New Castle, where he filled our rooms with his sweet songs for a few months. Then, one morning when I uncovered his cage, I found him dead. I couldn't believe it. Not until later did I find out what had probably killed him. On Dochet's he had drunk pure rainwater. At Fort Constitution the water was not only chlorinated by the city, but also by the army, and it was too much for poor Peter.

While at Portsmouth Harbor Light we subbed on Cape Neddick Light, also known as the Nubble, at York Beach, for several periods while the keeper, Mr. Brewster, took his vacation. A picturesque station, I think it was the most photographed one anywhere. On a high bluff, with a channel dividing it from the main-land, it is one of the few that is still occupied by a fam-ily.

I used to love to set the table for our lunch on the porch at Nubble, but I felt like a goldfish in a bowl as the tourists put the powerful telescope situated on the mainland on us and watched every move. Of course, they were not only watching us, but viewing the light too.

The first time Elson substituted for Mr. Brewster, a bachelor, we discovered he had a parrot. I thought, "Oh, oh, now I'll hear some not-so-good language." Elson was writing up his records in the office and we were laugh-ing and talking, when we heard a voice and laughter and thought it was visitors to see the light. But when we went out to see, we found it was the parrot mocking us.

The next morning I was getting breakfast and asked

Elson if he wanted coffee. A voice from the living room said, "I'd like coffee, Connie," as plain as I could have said it. Once the bird got into a noisy chattering, so Elson said he would stop him, and took his banjo into the living room and started playing. The parrot kept very quiet and when Elson finally started for the door hollered, "Come back here." To our surprise he liked the music and learned to stage a noisy chatter so Elson would play again. Not once in all the time we took care of him did he say a bad word.

I was pretty disturbed when I reached the Nubble and found that Mr. Brewster had a dog. He'd bought a harness for him in case we wanted to tie him outside, but the dog would wiggle out of that and be in the house before we could get back in after tying him. We had quite a time making him understand he could not be near me. He seemed puzzled, for he sensed that I liked him, yet did not dare let him love me. I felt bad, for he was a beautiful dog, but just the smell of him would give me asthma and make me violently ill.

My brother Carleton was officer in charge of Wood Island Coast Guard Station, about a mile from us out in the harbor. Shortly after we went to New Castle, we heard that the Coast Guard was to close Wood Island Station and move it in to our light. My brother verified it, and not long after he began to dismantle his station in readiness for its closing. He then went to be the officer in charge of Hampton Beach Coast Guard Station.

We began to look for a house to buy or rent, as I would have to move, while Elson stayed on at the station until he could retire. During that period houses to buy were scarce. We would have loved to stay in New Castle, but only one place was available and it was right up near a ledge with very little land, a thing I would be glad for today, but then Elson wanted land for gardens. Finally, we found a place in Eliot, Maine, only four miles from Portsmouth. I moved up there for the first time in September 1947.

The day we bought the house in Eliot, August 9, 1947, was a very important one to us. We had finally fulfilled one of our most cherished dreams and owned our own home. After the transfer of property, we returned to the light to find the Coast Guard construction engineer waiting with a three-man crew to begin converting the dwelling into a Coast Guard station. Indeed, my lovely mahogany table was already covered with construction dust. At two o'clock that day we received our orders to be moved by September 15, 1947.

The day we moved was a sad one for me. The last of our furniture and household effects were loaded aboard the Coast Guard truck, except the piano and dining room set which had to be moved by professional movers. Two young Coast Guardsmen perched on top of the furniture while Elson and I were in the cab. The two youngsters laughed and kidded, not understanding what a sad, uprooting event they were unconcernedly witnessing. A very happy chapter in my life was closing. I looked at Elson with tears I could not stop. He put his hand over mine and started the motor.

We drove by the fort walls and through the town of New Castle, waving to the families with whom we'd had pleasant times in the short period I was at Portsmouth Light. I knew we would miss the nice people of New Castle and the Fourth of July bonfire, the rug hooking classes, the church gatherings.

As it turned out, there was a delay in sending the Coast Guard crew to take over the light. Elson remained in charge for another year, so I rejoined him until I moved into the Eliot house for good in May of 1948. But my real leave-taking of lighthouse life was the day in 1947 when our furniture and I moved to Eliot. It was that day I said good-bye to a unique and happy part of my life, a life that was the life of so many of my family who served the Lifesaving Service, the Lighthouse Service, and finally the Coast Guard; a life of people risking their own lives to help men and ships; a life of order and duty.

EIGHT

RETIREMENT

Our home in Eliot was our first real home, and our last one. Elson had been on the water all his life and that was his love and vocation, but when he said good-bye to the sea he didn't want to go back again. So, he bought tractors and had a wonderful time planting vegetable gardens on our acre of land in Eliot.

We did a lot of work on the Eliot house. A two and a half story house, it was a cottage type with a large porch across the front. The front door opened on a reception hall with stairs on the left leading to the second floor. To the right of the hall was the living room and dining room; straight ahead was a room I turned into a den and breakfast room with a kitchen beyond that. Three bedrooms, each with a walk-in closet with window and light, and a bathroom filled the second floor. Two more rooms could be finished in the attic.

In high school I had been interested in design and had been particularly taken with a magazine picture of a room with a mural on the wall. I decided that if I ever had a home, I'd want my dining room decorated with a mural so I wouldn't feel closed in while I ate. Our new dining room was papered with an expensive wallpaper I wanted to keep, but it was too soiled. We took it off and painted the walls a soft, pinkish tan. I stood for a long time trying to get up the courage to paint a mural on the walls, but finally gave it up, feeling I was not that good an artist and could have made an awful mess of it.

But the bathroom was not as large, and on the tub wall I painted a heron standing in cattails, water flowing in from the sea. Several ducks, a boat tied to a pier, and a gull sitting on a piling completed the feeling of the seashore. I was quite proud of this room.

Some of the work on the house was done while I went back and forth to the light in the month before we moved our furniture in. But there was still much to do. That first day, the two Coast Guardsmen put all the upstairs furniture in one room and I made the sofa in the living room my bed. After Elson saw that I had enough to get by with, he and the others went back to the station though I could see he hated to leave me there in an upset house, not knowing anyone, everything strange. He called a couple of times in the evening to make sure I was all right, but it was the next evening before he could leave the station.

When he arrived he gave me a big box of goodies the cook had sent me as I had no way to shop. I'd put a small table in front of the fire burning in the fireplace, and we sat and ate our food like two lovebirds this first night in our own house.

In order to receive Social Security, Elson had to go into business for himself. He built two large henhouses and went into the chicken business in summer, raising 250 to 300 chickens, selling the eggs through the summer and the hens in the fall. We would then go to Florida for the winter, returning to Eliot about May first.

Elson also built sixteen-foot skiffs which he sold at the Trading Post in Kittery, where he sometimes worked. And he would contract exterior painting jobs. He never collected Social Security though I eventually was able to collect under it due to his work after retirement from lighthouses. In Eliot we joined the church and became part of the community. Elson was, of course, very musical and that made us especially welcome.

We started going to Florida in winter 1953/54 and continued until Elson's death in November 1960. One winter we spent in New Port Richey and the others in Lake Worth. One year Elson worked as a captain for a retired Standard Oil executive who lived on his yacht, but he didn't want to go to Pompano Beach where the man was moving the next year, though he liked him as an employer. Elson usually didn't like working for other people. He'd rather be his own boss and chose not to get into circumstances in life he didn't particularly care much about. Elson was happy doing as he did.

He particularly enjoyed playing for groups like the Boy Scouts at their one hundredth anniversary. He had all the boys participating, clapping as he played his banjo. I often accompanied him at the piano. Once we were invited to play for retired Navy nurses at a hospital and retirement home in Gulfport. I walked into the large room that reminded me of an English drawing room with highbacked chairs and beautiful appointments, and almost didn't dare to cross the floor to the grand piano. But I did and we played. We'd play waltzes and songs like "Ain't She Sweet," and Elson's favorite, "Somebody Stole My Gal."

I lost him to cancer on November 22, 1960, and I thought my life was over. We had been together, except for his war duty, for forty years lacking one day. I was holding his hand when he went and for the first time in my life realized how final death is. Never again would he speak to me or look at me over his glasses or tease me. Numb, I tried to think what I hadn't done to have kept him with me a while longer. I kissed him and went to my room where I was joined by my minister.

We laid Elson to rest near his mother and father in Bay View Cemetery in Larrabee.

I closed the house and went to Salisbury, Massachusetts, to be with my brother Carleton. He and his wife, Lydia, did all they could to help me, but the shock and loss were so great I couldn't sleep. Then one day, Carleton said, "Sis, how would you like to take a course at Newburyport High School?" He talked me into enrolling with him though it was forty-two years since I'd been inside a schoolhouse. This was the thing I needed. I returned to school with a vengeance and kept so busy I had no time to think.

I wondered what I'd do when I heard a banjo being played. The time came sooner than I expected. I had gone to the post office for stamps just before Christmas and was standing in the middle of a long line when the Christmas music stopped and a banjo with piano accompaniment came on playing the very music we had so often played together.

I felt as if a sharp knife were stabbing me, but I managed to control myself. I braced my feet and realized for the first time that I was completely alone now and I had to make my own decisions and my own life.

NINE

ON MY OWN

So, I went to work. My friend Olive Kimball was in charge of the children's department at Foye's Department Store in Portsmouth. She told the manager of the store about me and I was hired to work in the children's department. It was my first experience working with the public; I loved selling baby clothes to expectant mothers and Buster Brown outfits to doting grandparents. But I had to have serious surgery on my legs and had to leave.

Dr. Bunker, our old friend, then employed me, and knowing I loved anything historic and academic, encouraged me to try to find a position as head resident at a college. I sent out three applications, was interviewed at Farmington State College in Farmington, Maine, and accepted a position as a rotating head resident.

I felt like I was going home as I took the Auburn exit on Route 95 to Route 4. I had no Elson beside me and lighthouses seemed like a dream. I was leaving the sea far behind, my course now set for mountain country, so very different. These new occupations were interesting but I could never separate myself totally from the lighthouses and my life in them; they were embedded in my soul and my training in them a source of strength and courage. I was hoping this new life would be filled with as much fortitude and memories as precious.

There were butterflies in my stomach, but I couldn't let them stay, as my future depended on how well I performed my duties. I was alone and had to solve my own problems. At that moment I concentrated on my driving. Three years before, I had bought a new Rambler Classic with pushbutton shift, which I loved. It was deep blue with a white top, a pretty car.

I had never driven a car until 1960, when I was fifty-nine years old. That spring I awoke with the terrific feeling that I had to learn to drive our car. When I told Elson, he said, "I don't see any need as we always go together."

I said, "Well, Elson, we're driving to Florida and if you were taken sick I could at least get you to a hospital."

"All right, but you'll have to get someone to teach you."

I contacted the principal of the grammar school and took two lessons, but his hours and Elson's didn't agree, so I told Elson he would have to teach me. Everybody had told me never to let my husband teach me to drive, but he did, and when I finished with my driving test, the officer asked, "Who taught you to drive?" When I told him, he said, "He did an excellent job." Elson was tough on me, but it paid off. I never got to know his reaction to my driving because he passed away before he rode with me driving.

The ride into Farmington was beautiful as the bright sunny day gave a glow to the autumn foliage. Mount

Blue stretched its blue peak along the horizon surrounded by a red, gold, salmon, and green carpet. I drove around the campus to see if other head residents had arrived and since there was a car at each dorm, concluded that I was the last to come. I went to Mallet Hall where my apartment would be. The permanent head resident and Dean Williams were there to greet me. The dean had taken two rooms that joined and made a bedroom and an attractive living room for me. I was so pleased for I had thought I was to have just a bedroom.

I was still in a state of shock from my husband's death and was becoming resigned to the idea it would always be that way. But in the bedroom one night, just as the dormitory clock chimed twelve, I woke up feeling as though I had passed through a big, dark cloud and I seemed to hear a voice was saying, "You are all right. Just make the best of every day. All's well."

When a head resident had her two days off, I took her place, rotating among Stone, Mallet, and Dearborn Halls. I met and worked with many different personalities. It was one of the happiest years of my life and I still thank Doctor Bunker for giving me the courage to take on the job. Of course, Elson was with me, as always, but after the voice not as a sense of loss, but rather as a comfort and memory.

When college closed for the summer, I headed for my little apartment in Kittery, in the home of Willis and Ruth Parsons. The Parsons family had sort of adopted me, as my family members were long distances away, and I felt like I was going to my second home. I was elated because I was anxious to tell them the news that I was to be head resident of Dearborn Hall in the fall. The long drive seemed short for I knew these dear friends would be happy to share my joy.

Dearborn was a small dormitory for about forty-four junior and senior girls. I had a very nice year, easier than the first because I had become used to being responsible for so many people and had some good help, both from the rotating head resident and my desk girls.

Then, in January, Dean Williams fell on the ice and broke her hip. A few days later I had a surprise visit from Dr. Binley, Dean of Student Personnel, who handed me the following notice:

Official Notice
Academic and Administration

NOTICE: During the absence of Dean Williams, Mrs. Constance Small will assume responsibilities for the following areas in the Office of Student Personnel. Although the areas of responsibility may broaden, currently Mrs. Small will assume the following responsibilities:

1. Advisor to Inter Dorm Council

2. Authorize expenditures for women's organizations

3. Interview withdrawals and authorize them

4. Personal counseling for co-eds who request it or who may be referred to Mrs. Small

5. Supervise the Head Residents' rotating schedules

Mrs. Small will be available in the Office of Student Personnel, Monday through Friday from 1 P.M. to 4 P.M.

Dr. John Bingley
Dean of Student Personnel

I stood there holding the paper, thinking there must be some mistake. Finally I said, "Dr. Bingley, I'm not qualified for this. It can't be true."

He laughed and said, "It's no mistake. The college personnel and students have investigated you and chosen you." I thanked him and turned to hide the tears in my eyes at this honor.

The first day of my new responsibilities, I sat at Dean Williams' desk and thought, "I am in another world. It can't be me." But I saw the pile of papers on my desk and wrote out some memos to send in to Dr. Abbott, assistant to the president. The first memo came back ok'd, but a note at the bottom said, "You have a secretary. Use her." Reality hit me and I had a busy, interesting three months.

One memorable experience was the Deans' Conference at the University of Maine at Orono. Deans from all the colleges gathered to discuss how to find more productive solutions to problems that were getting more serious all the time. The opportunity to listen to these educators was helpful, for I still had my dormitory with all its problems to run.

The second summer vacation passed all too quickly as all vacations do.

I drove toward Mount Blue and onto the Farmington campus, noticing that the other head residents' cars were parked in the usual spots. We met with Dean Williams at the Pioneer Restaurant for dinner and a briefing on our fall schedules.

I'd been assigned as head resident of the new girls' dorm, Scott Hall South, named in honor of the retiring president of Farmington. Parking my car at the dorm, I looked up and down the long, three-story building realizing it was even larger than I had thought. In a few days, the three stories would be teeming with 169 girls. I hoped I could deal successfully with this job.

The first few weeks were busy with organizing the dormitory, changing rooms for those girls who were dissatisfied with their assigned rooms, and supervising fire drills, which were executed with quick, quiet responses until some prankster began pulling false ones, calling the other girls out of their sleep at all hours. I had some trouble adjusting, trying to match faces and names of so many girls and getting accustomed to the freshmen and sophomores, as well as the juniors and seniors I was used to.

Often freshmen girls came to my apartment asking if they could talk to me. I would ask what was bothering them and they told me their troubles, academic and personal. Often a girl would rise, put her arms around me, and say, "Thank you, Mother Small. You've helped me so much," and leave. I'd said nothing, just listened, but I was someone they could confide in.

The next year, when Dakin Hall was completed, I was chosen to be its head resident. I had as many girls there as at Scott South, but many I already knew since they transferred over from Scott.

Changes in rules made changes for the head residents in coping with problems. No longer did students have to sign in and out of the dormitory. Liquor was allowed in the dormitory and parietal hours allowed boys to visit the girls' rooms from seven to eleven o'clock in the evening. Inspection of rooms was discontinued, and girls who worked at the office desk were allowed to have boys in the office with them. Generally the dress code was lifted; this applied to the desk girls too.

When the dress code was lifted, I was asked by one of the girls how I felt about it. All I said was, "Well, if I was a business scout looking for promising young women to hire and I came to this office and saw a desk assistant, untidy, a can of beer in her hand, and her boyfriend's feet on the desk, I'd turn right around and never consider hiring her."

"You mean that, don't you, Mother Small?" she said, rather surprised.

"I certainly do," I said. But, bless their hearts, they were always neat, no beer or feet on the desk.

With all of these changes, I felt the place was falling apart. If so many of my girls hadn't been such nice young people, I'd have been very unhappy, but I was lucky and we had some fine meetings, social events, and discussions. There were very few times I wasn't proud of the dormitory.

One of those times occurred one evening when I was on desk duty. Hearing a loud noise in the hall, I went down the corridor, turned the corner, and stopped, shocked. Two girls were trying to get another girl, visibly drunk, upstairs to her room. They struggled to get her in her room before I saw her and in the struggle had knocked her down. They'd been to a special social event. This young girl was a replica of the painting I'd seen of the blue girl, dressed in a dainty blue dress, her hair in a ponytail tied by a ribbon with streamers down to her shoulders. She kept saying, "My head is hurting. Leave me alone."

Tears came to my eyes. Without saying a word I turned and went back to my desk. Here was the result of lifting the liquor rules and I felt sick for this sweet, dainty youngster I was sure had never been in this state before.

Two days later a knock came at my apartment door. When I opened it there stood the little blue girl, her face frightened, yet hopeful, as she asked if I would talk to her. I asked her to come in and sit down. She sat on the sofa, and for a time her head hung down as she struggled with herself. Finally she looked up and said, "I've been two days trying to get up courage enough to come see you. I am so ashamed about the other night. If my parents knew, they would have been so upset and shamed." She talked on hurriedly, showing a nervousness she was having difficulty controlling. I had observed this girl, mostly because she was so dainty and sweet, and I went over and put my arms around her. Big tears came streaming down her face as she said, "What are you going to do to me?"

"The only thing I'm going to do is to tell you this: if you could have been in my place and could have seen yourself as I saw you, you would never touch another drop of liquor again."

She looked at me in amazement and said, "You aren't going to scold or report me?"

"No, my dear, for I think you have experienced your own punishment. I admire the courage you've shown to come and talk with me."

She dried her tears. "Thank you, Mother Small. I'll never take another drink as long as I am here." To the best of my knowledge she never did.

I was particularly rewarded when girls told me I had helped them remain in college. When I retired, many of the girls brought me flowers, candy, and gifts. One came with a bouquet of field flowers she had picked in back of the dorm. She told me, "I don't have the money to buy you flowers or candy, so I went down in the field and picked these. I hope you like them." I was deeply touched and told her they were more precious because she gave me a part of herself. She was one of the girls who said I helped her to stay in college.

Seven wonderful years passed. Then, in 1971, I reached the retirement age of the college, so my own college days were over. On my last day, I checked the floors and basement of the dormitory. The students had left and the halls echoed with my footsteps.

My car was packed with all my belongings. As I locked the doors and gave the custodian the list of things to check, I felt sad to leave, for I loved Farmington and the friends I had made there, the college and the associations I had there.

I drove down Route 4 to Auburn, where I got on Route 95. As I passed through the tollgate, I bade farewell to another phase of my life. I was heading for my apartment in Kittery and wondered what course I would take from here.

Whenever I was on vacation I had gone over to say hello to Mr. Foye and the others I had worked with. One day after my retirement from Farmington, I went over and said jokingly to Mr. Foye, "I'm retired and free. I suppose you have my old job waiting for me?"

To my surprise, Mr. Foye said, "Take off your coat and go to work." Foye's was now a gift center and I loved the pretty things. I worked there for eight years. Then, since Mr. Parsons became ill and changes were taking place with him and Mrs. Parsons, and as new senior citizen housing was being built, I resigned from Foye's Gift Center and moved into the Foxwell Senior Citizens' complex in Kittery.

I belonged to several clubs. At one a woman asked me, "How on earth could anyone have any kind of a life in a lighthouse?" The question kept going around and around in my head until I decided, "Well, I don't know about anyone else's life, but I could tell them about ours and what we did to have an interesting one." I began to hunt up my old snapshot books and took them over to the Eagle Photo store to be made into slides. I showed the slides and told of our experiences, giving talks to different organizations. I had no idea my talks would gain the interest they have. I've given about seventy-five talks to church groups, newcomer clubs, museums, historical societies, and women's clubs. Many people have contacted me about articles they were writing about lighthouses and I've kept up a correspondence with them. I have been thrilled to contribute a unique bit of history and to have received so many rewarding results. It has kept me active and so far the rocking chair winks at me, but I do not heed.

As I open my drapes this morning, the rays of the rising sun dance through the trees and kiss the blossoms in the garden beneath my patio doors. The little chickadees chirp their thank-you for the seeds in their red feeder. I'm taken back to my lighthouse days when I went up in the tower and watched the day come to life. I still experience the joy this hour gave me.

May the sunrise give you hope and inspiration,
The sunset, the comfort of a day well spent.